W9-CMP-816

The Ultimate Guide to
MINECRAFT®
SERVER

Timothy L. Warner

QUE®

800 East 96th Street,
Indianapolis, Indiana 46240 USA

The Ultimate Guide to Minecraft Server

Copyright © 2016 by Que Publishing

ISBN-13: 978-0-7897-5457-8
ISBN-10: 0-7897-5457-6

Library of Congress Control Number: 2015939394

Printed in the United States of America

First Printing: July 2015

Trademarks

All terms mentioned in this book that are known to be trademarks or service marks have been appropriately capitalized. Que Publishing cannot attest to the accuracy of this information. Use of a term in this book should not be regarded as affecting the validity of any trademark or service mark.

Minecraft is a trademark of Mojang Synergies / Notch Development AB. This book is not affiliated with or sponsored by Mojang Synergies / Notch Development AB.

Warning and Disclaimer

Every effort has been made to make this book as complete and as accurate as possible, but no warranty or fitness is implied. The information provided is on an "as is" basis. The author and the publisher shall have neither liability nor responsibility to any person or entity with respect to any loss or damages arising from the information contained in this book

Special Sales

For information about buying this title in bulk quantities, or for special sales opportunities (which may include electronic versions; custom cover designs; and content particular to your business, training goals, marketing focus, or branding interests), please contact our corporate sales department at corpsales@pearsoned.com or (800) 382-3419.

For government sales inquiries, please contact governmentsales@pearsoned.com.

For questions about sales outside the U.S., please contact international@pearsoned.com.

Editor-in-Chief
Greg Wiegand

Executive Editor
Rick Kughen

Development Editor
William Abner

Managing Editor
Sandra Schroeder

Project Editor
Seth Kerney

Copy Editor
Cheri Clark

Indexer
Erika Millen

Proofreader
Jess DeGabriele

Technical Editor
John Baichtal

Editorial Assistant
Cindy Teeters

Book Designer
Mark Shirar

Compositor
Bronkella Publishing

Contents at a Glance

Introduction   1

CHAPTER 1   Minecraft Multiplayer from the Gamer's Perspective   5

CHAPTER 2   Building a Vanilla Minecraft Server   25

CHAPTER 3   Operating a Vanilla Minecraft Server   45

CHAPTER 4   Understanding Networking as It Relates to Minecraft   71

CHAPTER 5   Installing a Custom Minecraft Server   93

CHAPTER 6   Integrating Mods into Your Minecraft Server   113

CHAPTER 7   Exploring Minecraft Realms   137

CHAPTER 8   Taking Control of Minecraft with Third-Party Hosting   159

CHAPTER 9   Giving Your Players the Best Gaming Experience   185

CHAPTER 10   Monetizing Your Minecraft Server   209

APPENDIX   Tim's "Top 10" Lists   237

Index   247

Table of Contents

Introduction   1

Who Should Read This Book   1

How This Book Is Organized   2

Conventions Used in This Book   3

   Follow Me!   3

   About the Bitly Hyperlinks   3

System Requirements   4

Chapter 1   Minecraft Multiplayer from the Gamer's Perspective   5

Understanding Minecraft Multiplayer   6

   Minecraft Demo Mode Versus Minecraft Premium   7

   Please Avoid Cracked Launchers   8

   The Three Types of Minecraft Multiplayer   10

Finding "Good" Minecraft Servers   10

   Understanding Minecraft Server Lists   11

   A Word on Minecraft Minigames   14

   About Connection Addresses   15

   Public Versus Whitelist Servers   15

Joining an Online Server   16

Minecraft Multiplayer Netiquette   19

   The Importance of Help   19

   Chatting with OPs and Other Players   20

   Setting Chat Options   22

   The Three Rules of Multiplayer Netiquette   23

      Rule #1: Obey the Server Rules—Or Leave   23

      Rule #2: Act in Accordance with the "Golden Rule"   23

      Rule #3: Ask Without Fear   24

The Bottom Line   24

Chapter 2   Building a Vanilla Minecraft Server   25

Preparing the Java Environment   25

Verifying Your Java Version (Windows)   26

Verifying Your Java Version (OS X)   27

Downloading and Installing the JRE   27

Installing the Minecraft Server   28

The Windows Installation Process   29

The OS X Installation Process   31

An Interlude...Your Lab Environment   34

Buy Another Copy of Minecraft? Really?   34

First Run and Initial Configuration Steps   34

Understanding the Server Configuration Files   35

The Minecraft Server Console   37

Running More Than One Server Instance   42

Finding Vanilla Servers on the Internet   43

The Bottom Line   44

Chapter 3   Operating a Vanilla Minecraft Server   45

Understanding Our Test Environment   45

Configuring the Server's World   47

Introducing Sublime Text   47

Understanding **server.properties**   48

Getting Your User(s) Connected   50

Scanning, Scanning...   51

Interacting with Your Users   53

/say, **/tell**, and **/me**   55

/tp and **/give**   59

Exerting Discipline on Your Server   59

/kick   60

/ban and **/ban-ip**   61

/pardon, **/pardon-ip**, and **/whitelist**   63

Adding a Management Layer to Your Server   65

Introducing McMyAdmin   65

Installation Notes   67

Configuration Notes   67

McMyAdmin Editions   68

Opening a Single-Player Game to the LAN   68

The Bottom Line   70

Chapter 4   Understanding Networking as It Relates to Minecraft   71

Revisiting Our Test Network   72

Learning as We Go: Basic Networking Terminology   73

IP Addresses   73

Private and Public Addresses   74

Network Address Translation   75

DHCP   75

Taking the Next Step: Preparing Our Network for Minecraft Server   76

Discovering Our Computer's Networking Configuration   76

Viewing Our Router's Configuration   78

Allowing Minecraft Traffic Through the Firewall   81

Ports   81

Configuring Port Forwarding   83

Testing the Connection   85

Let's Play!   86

Using a Hostname Instead of an IP Address   88

Understanding DNS and DDNS   88

Setting Up No-IP   88

Sweeping Up the Shavings   90

The Bottom Line   91

Chapter 5   Installing a Custom Minecraft Server   93

Beginnings: It's a Wild, Wild West   93

If Not Bukkit, Then What?   94

Installing SpigotMC   95

Starting SpigotMC Server   96

Configuring SpigotMC   97

`server.properties`   98

`spigot.yml`   98

`bukkit.yml`   98

Testing the Player Experience   99

Introducing Bukkit Plugins   100

Describing the Most Popular Plugins   100

A Question of Balance   102

Installing, Configuring, and Using Bukkit Plugins   102

Obtaining Essentials: RTFM   102

Configuring Essentials   106

Testing the Gameplay Experience   108

The Bottom Line   112

Chapter 6   Integrating Mods into Your Minecraft Server   113

Introducing Cauldron   113

Minecraft Forge in a Nutshell   114

Installing the Forge Client   115

Getting Cauldron Up and Running   117

First, Our Plugin Proof of Concept   118

PermissionsEx Quick Start   118

Testing the Plugin   120

Now for the Good Stuff—Installing a Mod   122

Installing RailCraft   122

Testing the Railcraft Player Experience   125

Experimenting with Integrated Modpacks and Launchers   129

Feed the Beast (FTB)   130

Installing FTB Server   132

Starting the FTB Launcher   134

ATLauncher and Other Options   134

Quality Client Mods   135

The Bottom Line   136

Chapter 7   Exploring Minecraft Realms   137

Understanding Cloud Services   137

Pros and Cons   139

Introducing Minecraft Realms   139

Let's Sign Up!   140

Playing in a Minecraft Realms World   142

    Inviting Players   145

    Managing Players   148

A Brief Tutorial on Command Blocks   150

    About Target Selectors   151

    Programming Command Blocks   152

Configuring Minecraft Realms   154

    Backup and Restore   154

    Viewing Backups   154

    Forcing a Backup   155

    Downloading a World to Single-Player   155

    Uploading a World to Realms   156

    Restoring a World   157

The Bottom Line   157

Chapter 8   Taking Control of Minecraft with Third-Party Hosting   159

What to Look for in a Third-Party Minecraft Host   160

    Minecraft Hosting Terminology   160

    What's Important in a Minecraft Host   161

Joining MCProHosting   163

Getting to Know the Control Panel   168

    Configuring and Starting Our Minecraft Server   169

    Logging In   170

    Adding Some Plugins   172

Making Additional Tweaks to Your Server   175

    Editing Your Config Files   175

    Deploying a Resource Pack   177

Mapping Your Server to a Domain   180

    Domain Name Mapping with GoDaddy   180

A Brief Roster of Other Well-Regarded Minecraft Hosting Companies   183

The Bottom Line   184

Chapter 9   Giving Your Players the Best Gaming Experience   185

Protecting Your Server from Abuse   186

Distributed Denial-of-Service Attack   186

What to Do to Prevent DDoS Attacks   187

Griefing   188

Hack Yourself   189

Blocking Griefers   190

Tips for Addressing Griefers   194

Customizing the World Spawn   194

Setting the Server Spawn   195

Building a Spawn Lobby   196

Preparing the Land for a Lobby Schematic   197

WorldEdit—A More Flexible Terraforming Solution   199

Using WorldEdit to Drop in a Schematic   200

Supporting Multiple Worlds and Teleportation   202

Using Multiverse   202

Creating and Teleporting Between Worlds   203

Deploying Portals   203

Connecting the Two Worlds   206

The Bottom Line   208

Chapter 10   Monetizing Your Minecraft Server   209

Understanding Mojang's Position on Minecraft Server Monetization   210

The New Minecraft EULA   210

The Backlash Against Mojang   211

Monetizing Minecraft While Maintaining EULA Compliance   212

Donations   212

In-Game Advertising and Sponsorship   216

Cosmetic Upgrade Sales   217

VIP Server Access or Subscriptions   219

Setting Up BuyCraft   220

Creating a Paid Package   223

Giving a Paid Item to All Players   225

Creating a Free Package   226

Advertising Your Minecraft Server   228

Where to Advertise   228

The Importance of the Server Status Banner   229

Registering Your Minecraft Server   231

About Voting   232

Someplace to Compare Yourself   233

Creating a Custom Server Entry for the Minecraft Client   234

Customizing the MOTD   235

Final Thoughts   235

Appendix   Tim's "Top 10" Lists   237

Top 10 Minecraft Hosts   237

Top 10 Public Minecraft Servers   239

Top 10 Bukkit Plugins   240

Top 10 Modpacks   240

Top 10 Resource/Texture Packs   242

Top 10 Minecraft YouTubers   243

Top 10 Minecraft Minigames   243

Top 10 Minecraft Custom Maps   244

Top 10 Minecraft Seeds   245

Index   247

About the Author

Timothy Warner is an IT professional and technical trainer based in Nashville, Tennessee. Tim became acquainted with information technology in 1982 when his dad bought the family a Timex Sinclair 1000 home computer and he taught himself BASIC programming. Today he works as an author/evangelist for Pluralsight and shares Windows PowerShell knowledge with anyone who'll listen at his Two Minute PowerShell blog: http://2minutepowershell. com. You can reach Tim directly via LinkedIn: http://linkedin.com/in/timothywarner.

Dedication

To my favorite Minecraft buddies: Xander, Xan, Luther, Daisy, and Zoey. Watch out for those Creepers!

Acknowledgments

Thanks to Markus Persson and the Mojang team for giving the world Minecraft. You guys must know in your hearts the huge impact the game has had on all of us. Thanks also to the entire third-party Minecraft community—you folks inspire me to be a better gamer, a better sysadmin, and a better programmer.

It may take a village to raise a child, but I know that it takes a large office full of talented professionals to publish a book. To that end, I want to thank my editor Rick Kughen for never doubting my abilities even when I doubted them myself. Thanks to my publisher, Greg Wiegand, for being so willing to embrace my sometimes wacky ideas.

Editorial and production staff rarely receive the credit they deserve. Thanks so much to John Baichtal, my technical editor, and to Cheri Clark, my copy editor, for making my writing as clean and accurate as it can be. I extend my gratitude as well to Seth Kerney, my production editor, and to the ever-helpful Kristen Watterson for streamlining the book publishing process.

Thanks to my family and friends for your love and encouragement. Finally and most importantly, thank you, my reader! I hope that this book takes your Minecraft gaming to the next level, and possibly serves as a springboard for new hobbies and career opportunities.

We Want to Hear from You!

As the reader of this book, *you* are our most important critic and commentator. We value your opinion and want to know what we're doing right, what we could do better, what areas you'd like to see us publish in, and any other words of wisdom you're willing to pass our way.

We welcome your comments. You can email or write to let us know what you did or didn't like about this book—as well as what we can do to make our books better.

Please note that we cannot help you with technical problems related to the topic of this book.

When you write, please be sure to include this book's title and author as well as your name and email address. We will carefully review your comments and share them with the author and editors who worked on the book.

Email: feedback@quepublishing.com

Mail: Que Publishing
        ATTN: Reader Feedback
        800 East 96th Street
        Indianapolis, IN 46240 USA

Reader Services

Visit our website and register this book at quepublishing.com/register for convenient access to any updates, downloads, or errata that might be available for this book.

Introduction

> **"Success is a journey, not a destination. The doing is often more important than the outcome."**
> **—Arthur Ashe, legendary professional tennis player**

Hello, and welcome to Minecraft server training! I invested dozens of hours in the Minecraft single-player game before I found the joy of multiplayer. Because I've been a fan of first-person shooter (FPS) games since Wolfenstein 3D (remember that one?), I enjoy player vs. player (PvP) matches in shared Minecraft worlds.

I've also been a bit of a nerd regarding role-playing games (RPGs); again, I can have this in Minecraft multiplayer by exploring and building with friends from all over the world.

This book, however, isn't so much about the multiplayer player's experience (although I devote a chapter to that subject). Instead, I'm going to teach you everything you need to know to build and maintain your very own Minecraft server, from soup to nuts. Are you excited? You should be!

Who Should Read This Book

As an author, I always write with my three primary audiences in mind:

- **Potential Minecraft Server Admins:** Perhaps you've experimented with hosting a Minecraft server and gotten bogged down in all the details. *Hint:* Most YouTube "instructors" don't know how to instruct at all. You're reading this book so that you can get clear, easy-to-follow directions to set up an awesome Minecraft server.

- **Geeky Types:** You're the kind of person who digested my *Hacking Raspberry Pi* book (http://www.amazon.com/Hacking-Raspberry-Pi-Timothy-Warner/dp/0789751569) in one sitting. You intend to leverage your new Minecraft server skills to become familiar with computer networking and network security for other purposes (maybe building a new career!).

- **Teachers and Students:** I'm both a teacher and a student, so I know more than most about how useful Minecraft is as an educational tool. You can learn to do computer programming by building Minecraft mods and Bukkit plug-ins. You can learn how to set up and manage computer networks by hosting your own Minecraft server.

If you find that you don't belong in any of the previous three classifications, don't worry about it. Set your sights on learning as much as you can and, above all else, having fun, and you'll be fine!

How This Book Is Organized

I always write books in such a way that you'll derive maximum benefit by reading the chapters in order. With no further buildup, allow me to present the chapter-by-chapter details on how I structured the content:

- Chapter 1, "Minecraft Multiplayer from the Gamer's Perspective," brings new Minecraft multiplayer gamers up to speed with how the game works and how to navigate within its worlds.

- In Chapter 2, "Building a Vanilla Minecraft Server," you learn how to use Mojang's own authorized Minecraft server. I give you instructions for both Windows and OS X systems.

- In Chapter 3, "Operating a Vanilla Minecraft Server," you take your understanding of the official Minecraft server to the next level. Although the platform is limited, take heart because you'll apply all your newfound skills to custom servers later in the book.

- In Chapter 4, "Understanding Networking as It Relates to Minecraft," you master the fundamentals of data networking. This is a huge subject, to be sure. However, I give you what you need to host your own Minecraft server with confidence.

- In Chapter 5, "Installing a Custom Minecraft Server," you move off the Mojang reservation and embrace Minecraft server third-party development. You'll get up to speed with what's what in the often-confusing and ever-volatile world of Bukkit, Spigot, and other server platforms.

- In Chapter 6, "Integrating Mods into Your Minecraft Server," you begin to understand how we can broaden and deepen our Minecraft server's feature set by deploying mods. Again, this can be a confusing subject to tackle on your own, but you're in good hands with me!

- In Chapter 7, "Exploring Minecraft Realms," you learn how to use Mojang's "other" officially licensed server. Realms is a cloud-based service, which means that you're saved from most of the back-end configuration that you're responsible for when you host your server inside your home.

- In Chapter 8, "Taking Control of Minecraft with Third-Party Hosting," you learn how you can combine the flexibility of third-party unofficial Minecraft servers with the stability, security, and reliability of a cloud server such as Realms.

- In Chapter 9, "Giving Your Players the Best Gaming Experience," you pick up best-practice tips for staying focused on your player base, avoiding server damage through griefing, and ensuring that players want to stay on your server for a long time to come.

- In Chapter 10, "Monetizing Your Minecraft Server," you learn what options you have for recouping server costs while staying within the bounds of the Mojang end user license agreement (EULA).

Conventions Used in This Book

In my experience as an author and a teacher, I've found that many readers and students skip over this part of the book. Congratulations for reading it! Doing so will pay off in big dividends because you'll understand how and why we formatted this book the way that we did.

Follow Me!

Throughout the book, you'll find "Follow Me!" exercises, which are opportunities for you to apply what you're learning right then and there in the book. I do believe in knowledge stacking, so you can expect that later "Follow Me!" exercises assume that you know how to do stuff that you did in previous exercises.

Therefore, your best bet is to read each chapter in sequence and work through every "Follow me!" exercise.

About the Bitly Hyperlinks

Whenever I want to point you to an Internet resource to broaden and deepen the content you're learning, I provide a uniform resource locator (URL, also called an Internet address) in the following form:

http://bit.ly/uaKpYD

You might wonder what the heck this is. The way I look at it, if I were reading this title as a print book and needed to type out a URL given to me by the author, I would rather type in a "shortie" URL than some long, crazy URL with all sorts of special characters. *The most important thing I have to tell you concerning the bit.ly short URLs is that the ending part is case sensitive.* Therefore, typing the previous URL as, say, http://bit.ly/UaKpyD isn't going to get you to the same page as what I intended.

System Requirements

You don't need a heck of a lot, computer-wise, to work through all the procedures I provide in this book. Let me give you the run-down:

- **A Windows or Mac computer:** As I'm sure you know, Minecraft runs on just about every hardware platform known to humankind. However, I've found the multiplayer experience in the "classic" Windows and OS X versions to be the most flexible and full-featured. As I said earlier, I give you all instructions for both Macs and Windows computers.

- **An Internet connection:** This requirement should be a no-brainer. After all, how can you host an Internet-accessible Minecraft multiplayer server unless you have a live connection to the Internet!

- **Basic computer navigational skills:** If you're worried about having to know Java programming to learn Minecraft server, don't be. We aren't developing Minecraft mods here, after all. That said, you'll need to know how to move around your computer, create folders, copy files, and create, edit, and save text files.

Okay—that's enough of the preliminaries. It's time to learn how to do Minecraft multiplayer!

1

"It is said that if you know your enemies and know yourself, you will not be imperiled in a hundred battles; if you do not know your enemies but do know yourself, you will win one and lose one; if you do not know your enemies nor yourself, you will be imperiled in every single battle."

—Sun Tzu, The Art of War

Minecraft Multiplayer from the Gamer's Perspective

What You'll Learn in This Chapter:

- How Minecraft multiplayer works
- How to purchase Minecraft Premium edition to unlock multiplayer capabilities
- How to find the best Minecraft servers on the Internet
- How to navigate and behave on online Minecraft servers

To be an effective Minecraft server administrator, you need to possess a deep understanding of the multiplayer game itself. To that end, my goal as your instructor is to equip you with all the background knowledge you need in order to have a great time finding and playing Minecraft multiplayer.

Even if you've spent time playing on public or private servers, I'm sure that you'll pick up some useful information along the way. I've met server operators who barely understand the rules of Minecraft, much less how to actually play single-player or multiplayer. That's a big mistake! Minecraft is a game, after all, because we're supposed to have fun with it.

Let's get to work.

Understanding Minecraft Multiplayer

The Minecraft single-player game has five modes:

- **Survival:** The player must gather all materials to survive.
- **Creative:** The player is given all game assets and cannot die.
- **Adventure:** The player can break blocks only with appropriate tools.
- **Hardcore:** Game difficulty is set to "Hard" and the world map is deleted if the player dies.
- **Spectator:** The player exists in the game world as a "ghost" and cannot interact with any game assets.

Although I enjoy playing the Xbox One Minecraft version the most, you have maximum flexibility when you play the Windows or OS X versions. In this book, we'll limit our discussion of Minecraft multiplayer to only those platforms.

As you can see in Figure 1.1, you can access the multiplayer game in licensed Minecraft directly from the home screen.

FIGURE 1.1 Single-player is fun, but many players believe that the real action occurs in multiplayer Minecraft.

NOTE

Even though we assume you're playing the Windows or OS X Minecraft in this book, you should be able to apply much of what you learn, from the player's viewpoint anyway, to other Minecraft versions.

Minecraft Demo Mode Versus Minecraft Premium

Anybody can visit minecraft.net and download a copy of Minecraft "for fun and for free," as they say. However, the free version has the following limitations:

- Player is restricted to Survival mode.
- The world map is fixed and generates by using the same seed.
- Game time is limited to five in-game days (which equals 1 hour, 40 minutes in clock time).
- Public multiplayer functionality is disabled.

The last point in the previous list should give you concern. The bottom line is that if you plan to play Minecraft Multiplayer, you need to purchase a game license.

FOLLOW ME!

Purchase a Minecraft License

In this exercise, we'll purchase a Minecraft license and download the software. To buy Minecraft, you'll need (a) an acceptable form of payment; (b) an Internet connection; and (c) a Windows or OS X computer that meets the game's minimum system requirements. To view those system requirements, visit the following Mojang Support page: https://help.mojang.com/customer/portal/articles/325948.

1 Point your web browser to http://minecraft.net and click Register in the top right-hand part of the web page.

2 Create your Mojang account by supplying a real email address, a strong password, and your date of birth. Click Create Account when you're finished.

3 Click the link in the Mojang verification email message that should arrive at your inbox within mere seconds.

4 In the Account Options web page, enter your desired Minecraft username. Think long and hard about this decision because you cannot change your username and it will be unique among all the millions of Minecraft players around the world.

5 Fill in your payment details. As of this writing, Mojang accepts the standard credit/ debit cards of PayPal as valid payment methods. At the moment, a single-user Minecraft license costs $26.95 USD. Click Purchase, and you'll be whisked back to the Minecraft. net home page. This time you'll see a big ol' Download button—click that.

6 Figure 1.2 is the sparse Minecraft Download page. The website will detect whether you're running Microsoft Windows or Apple OS X and will offer you the correct product version.

7 To install Minecraft, simply open the `.dmg` archive and drag `Minecraft.app` into your Mac's `Application` folder. On Windows systems, double-click the `.exe` installer and follow the instructions.

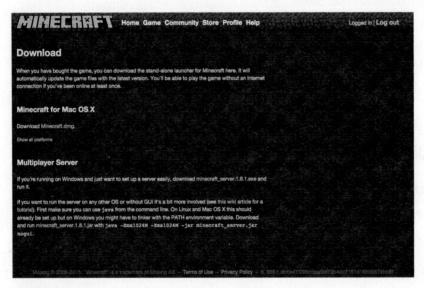

FIGURE 1.2   After you've purchased a license, you can redownload the Minecraft launcher as many times as you want. Note that Mojang's "vanilla" Minecraft server is hosted on this page as well.

Please Avoid Cracked Launchers

It's important to note that when you download Minecraft, you're not actually downloading the game itself. Instead you're downloading the launcher, which is the "engine" behind the single-player and multiplayer games. Therefore, Mojang knows that you legally purchased a license for the game because you're required to log in every time you start the launcher.

To that point, in today's world of rampant software piracy, some Minecraft users opt to download modified ("cracked") game launchers that let them play the full single-player and multiplayer modes for free. Please avoid this! Besides the obvious reason that using pirated software constitutes theft, you also make yourself vulnerable to the following hazards:

- Cracked Minecraft launchers are popular targets for malicious software that can damage your computer or steal your identity. Malicious users like to exploit Minecraft because so many people around the world play the game.

- If Mojang or an ethical Minecraft server operator detects that you're running an illegal copy of the game, they can and likely will "blacklist" your Mojang user account and/or computer's IP address.

- If your Internet service provider (ISP) detects that you've downloaded pirated software, you run the risk of them suspending or terminating your Internet service

The obvious question is, "How can I tell whether I'm running a cracked or legitimate Minecraft launcher?" The answer is that as long as you only ever download the launcher directly from mojang.net, then you're safe. If, by contrast, you download a launcher from any other website, then you're at risk.

Take a look at Figure 1.3; one glance at the title bar and completely nonstandard launcher interface should tell you to run the other way (read: uninstall the software completely) and fast.

FIGURE 1.3 The individuals who make illegal cracked Minecraft launchers generally don't take pains to hide their work; in most cases you can almost immediately detect cracked launchers.

The Three Types of Minecraft Multiplayer

Perhaps you've invested several (or several hundred) hours playing the Minecraft single-player game. Now you want to step up to the big leagues and give Minecraft multiplayer a try. What's available?

First of all, let's go ahead and formally define Minecraft multiplayer. A multiplayer Minecraft world is a world that exists not (necessarily) on your own computer, but on another computer called a server. More than one player can work within that single, shared world. Players can chat with each other by using text messages, and the types of specific gameplay that are available depend on a number of factors that we'll discuss in detail throughout the rest of this book. That's basically Minecraft multiplayer in a nutshell.

Now let me introduce you to the Minecraft game types:

The **online server** multiplayer game is the type that most Minecraft users focus on. Here multiple players log on to the same Minecraft server, which is publicly reachable over the Internet. By the end of this chapter you'll know all about locating, connecting to, and playing on online Minecraft servers.

The **local area network** (LAN) server is a Minecraft server that you or someone else makes available on a private network. For instance, you and your friends might join a shared Minecraft world hosted on a server located on your school campus. By the end of this book, you'll understand how to set up your own LAN server and participate in local network Minecraft multiplayer games.

Minecraft Realms is a subscription service offered by Mojang that helps people host their own Minecraft servers without having all the requisite background knowledge. By the end of this book, you'll have a clear picture as to how Realms works. However, I'm confident you'll never use Realms because you'll instead prefer the flexibility of hosting and managing your own Minecraft server your way. Besides, Realms worlds support only 10 simultaneously connected players, and I know you want to manage a server hosting hundreds of sessions, am I right?

Now let's turn our attention to the all-important question of precisely how we can find quality online Minecraft servers to join and have some fun with.

Finding "Good" Minecraft Servers

With a game as enormously popular as Minecraft, there is no shortage of public Minecraft servers out on the Internet. Your challenge is to separate the wheat from the chaff and find good, quality servers.

You're likely to have your eyes cross and your brain overload if you simply run a Google search for "good Minecraft servers." It's crazy how many Minecraft servers exist, and equally crazy how many of them are pure junk.

We'll get into this later in the book, but Mojang, the creators and owners of Minecraft before Microsoft bought them in 2014, shook up the multiplayer world when they changed the game's end user license agreement (EULA, pronounced "YOU-lah") in June 2014.

The EULA change prohibited Minecraft server operators from charging real-world cash for in-game currency, prohibited them from charging for access to core in-game elements, and insisted that server operators make it clear that their servers are in no way, shape, or fashion authorized or in any way affiliated with Mojang.

Perhaps you want to get into the Minecraft server hosting game for profit? According to the current EULA, which Microsoft might likely change in the future, you can still legally take the following actions:

- Charge players to access your server
- Accept voluntary donations
- Provide in-game advertising and/or server sponsorship opportunities
- Sell in-game items that aren't central to core gameplay

I mention all this up front because you'll definitely be able to spot which Minecraft online servers are set up for profit and which are set up for the joy of the game.

Understanding Minecraft Server Lists

I'm not afraid to give you suggestions for finding the best Minecraft servers because I am a committed Minecraft gamer and server operator myself. For my money, the most reliable and reputable Minecraft server lists are the ones located at the Minecraft Forum (http://minecraftforum.net). Be advised that the Minecraft Forum is not owned or affiliated with Mojang or Microsoft. That said, I believe it's one of the most highly rated and reputable Minecraft community sites.

From the Minecraft Forum home page, click Servers from the top navigation bar. Your best bet is to fill out relevant filter fields with your preferences and perform a targeted search. Take a look at Figure 1.4 and I'll show you what you need to know to successfully navigate this page.

FIGURE 1.4   The Minecraft Forum (http://minecraftforum.net) The Servers page has a rich search interface to help you find only Minecraft servers that meet your specifications.

A: Choose either your own country from this list, or one that's nearby. You want the fastest possible performance and the lowest possible latency (delay), so geographical distance counts.

B: It seems obvious that you'd want to find only servers that are currently online, right?

C: You'll learn soon enough that most Minecraft servers have plugins that broaden gameplay and make the server easier to administer; to start out I'd suggest that you leave this field blank.

D: I'm a "family-friendly" Minecraft guy, so I tend to stick with G or PG-rated servers. In general, family-friendly servers prohibit swearing and other behaviors that aren't suitable for younger players.

E: Again, why you'd choose to look at full servers is beyond me, but the search option exists. Some Minecraft players prefer smaller, more intimate servers, whereas other players love 'em big.

F: We'll discuss the different Minecraft server game types momentarily; leaving this field empty locates all servers.

G: In the search results, you should sort the Ping field in ascending order. Lower values here mean faster server connections and a better gameplay experience.

H: This fraction gives you a good indication of how full a server is.

Go ahead and run some searches and see what you can find. When you click a Minecraft server in the results list, you'll see a page that's similar to what you see in Figure 1.5.

NOTE

Some Minecraft server lists also include server uptime. This value, expressed as a percentage, gives you an indication of how stable a particular server is. Servers with lower uptimes tend to be machines that are (typically) served out of someone's bedroom as opposed to an honest-to-goodness data center. Obviously, higher uptime numbers are preferred here.

FIGURE 1.5 Good Minecraft server operators take the time to write a quality advertisement to attract as many players as possible. Look for a link to a dedicated website, and, of course, the server connection address.

Figure 1.5 is an advertisement for a particular server. You'll find great variety here—some server operators are detail-oriented and provide a summary of the server's philosophy, which plugs are available, and of course the connection address.

By contrast, some server operators provide nothing other than the name of the server and the connection address. You don't want to be like them!

TIP

Every decision you make concerning your Minecraft server should be based on this consideration: "Does this action help my players?"

A Word on Minecraft Minigames

Over the past couple of years, the Minecraft multiplayer community has developed a number of themed minigames that actually constitute a game within a game environment. Some servers are entirely dedicated to a particular gameplay mode; other servers are big enough that they have several worlds devoted to each minigame type.

Here is a list of the most popular Minecraft multiplayer minigames:

Anarchy: Anything goes—there are no rules.

Capture the Flag: Two or more teams compete to capture a centrally located flag or other item.

City: Players work and "live" cooperatively in a large-scale Minecraft village.

Cops and Robbers: Some players are the cops, and they chase other players who are the robbers.

Economy: Server includes popular economy-oriented mods such as iConomy, MultiCurrency, eWallet, and so forth.

Faction/Team PvP: Players can form and join clans to compete against each other.

Feed the Beast: Server includes the "Feed the Beast" modpack.

Hardcore PvP: Players have only one life, and when they die, they receive temporary or permanent bans from the server.

Hunger Games: Players compete in a "one Steve standing" fashion similar to the *Hunger Games* books and movies.

Parkour: In this minigame, pronounced "par-KOOR," players use innovative jumping moves to complete challenges.

Player versus Player (PvP): Players battle each other in a manner similar to popular first-person shooter (FPS) games.

Player versus Environment (PvE): Players work together or separately to defeat mobs.

Prison: Players take the role of jailers or prisoners, with the latter's objective being escaping the prison.

Skyblock: Players spawn on a floating island and complete survival challenges with limited resources.

Tekkit: Server includes some of the best technology-oriented mods: IndustrialCraft, RailCraft, BuildCraft, and the like.

About Connection Addresses

You'll learn all you ever wanted to know about domain name system (DNS) and IP addresses soon enough. For now, all you need to know is that you use a Minecraft server's connection address to join that server. For example, referring to Figure 1.5, note that the connection address mc.betadev.co.uk allows us to join the BetaDev server.

In time you'll become more familiar with DNS top-level domain (TLD) names; for example, the .uk name tells us that the BetaDev server is located in the United Kingdom.

Public Versus Whitelist Servers

The sad truth is that some players simply don't play well with others. For example, griefing will likely cause you, well, grief. *Griefing* refers to any form of harassment in a Minecraft multiplayer game.

To make it tougher for griefers to get into a world and create havoc, some server administrators require that prospective players register a user account on their public website. These registration-only servers are known as whitelist servers.

The best Minecraft servers are those that have a dedicated community and an active website. Take a look at the cubeville.org public server in Figure 1.6.

TIP

You should always make your Minecraft server rules highly visible on your website. This way no player can ever accuse you of not telling him or her "the rules." Moreover, you have an easy link to share with your users to guide them toward those rules.

FIGURE 1.6 Quality Minecraft servers like Cubeville typically have their own website and active community.

Joining an Online Server

Assuming that you have a live Internet connection, a licensed copy of Minecraft, and a multiplayer server connection address, let's get this party started and join a multiplayer game!

FOLLOW ME!

Join an Online Minecraft Server

In this exercise, we'll join Cubeville, one of the Internet's most highly respected family-friendly Minecraft servers.

1. Open a web browser and navigate to cubeville.org. Then verify that the server status is "online" and the population isn't full (you can see this information in Figure 1.6). While you're at the site, please read Cubeville's rules, check out the map, and investigate the forums. Cubeville is one of the best-documented online Minecraft servers I've ever seen.

2 Note that the Cubeville server, at least as of this writing in spring 2015, runs Minecraft v1.7.2. You'll find that Minecraft server versions often fall behind the latest public Minecraft release. The good news is that the Minecraft launcher allows us to start any version of the game we need or want.

3 Start the Minecraft launcher and log in with your Mojang username and password.

4 In the lower-left corner of the launcher, click Edit Profile; this opens the Minecraft Profile Editor, shown in Figure 1.7.

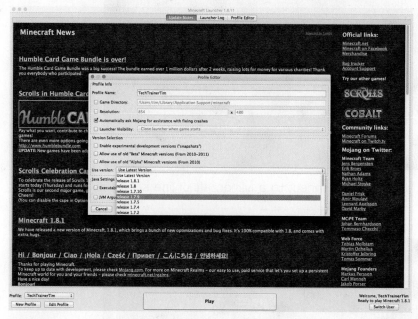

FIGURE 1.7   We use the Minecraft profile editor to play game versions that are compatible with a target server.

5 In the Profile Editor, open the Use Version drop-down and select release 1.7.2. Observe that the launcher defaults to using the latest public-release Minecraft version by default. Click Save Profile to return to the launcher.

6 Verify that the launcher says "Ready to play Minecraft 1.7.2" in the lower right, and then click Play to enter the game proper.

7 From the Minecraft home screen, click Multiplayer.

8 In the Play Multiplayer screen, click Add Server.

9 Type in a friendly name for the server and enter the connection address (Cubeville's is easy: cubeville.org). As you can see in Figure 1.8, I like keeping things simple. Click Done to continue.

10 Study all the wonderful server status info the Play Multiplayer screen provides. As you see in Figure 1.9, the connection bars indicate the strength/speed of your connection; the more bars (five out of five is the max), the better your connection to that server.

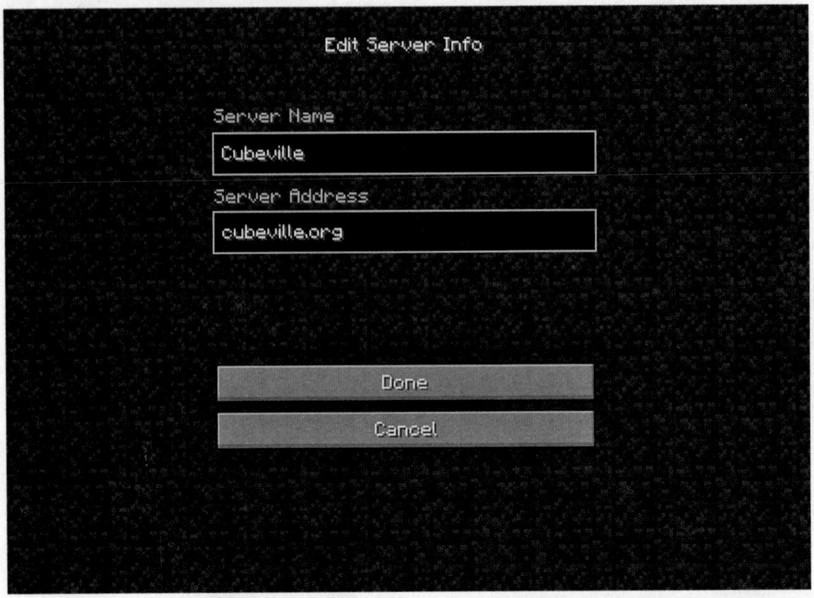

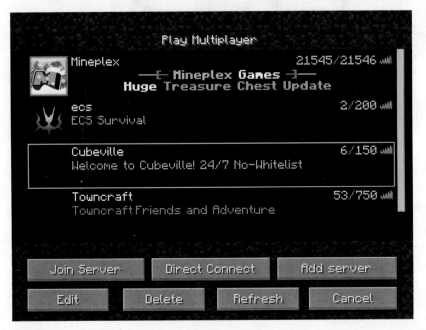

FIGURE 1.8 All you need to connect to a Minecraft online server is a name and a connection address.

FIGURE 1.9 The Play Multiplayer screen gives you excellent "at a glance" information regarding your stored Minecraft servers. Take note of connection bars, the number of free player slots, and Minecraft version dependencies.

The fraction tells you how many users are currently logged on versus the total number of player slots on that server.

11 Double-click the Cubeville entry to enter the server. Fasten your seatbelt and prepare to have fun!

TIP

You can use the Profile Editor to save more than one profile. What I do is have a profile for different Minecraft versions that correspond to the versions that my favorite servers run. This makes it more streamlined to join different servers.

As Figure 1.10 shows, your Minecraft client will display an error message if you try to connect to a server that has version and/or other requirements that aren't met by your current setup.

FIGURE 1.10 Running an incompatible Minecraft client version is the most common reason for seeing connection status errors.

Minecraft Multiplayer Netiquette

Netiquette, pronounced "NET-ih-KETT," is the Internet version of etiquette. Basically we're talking about nothing more than having good manners. Before we get into that, though, I want to make sure you're comfortable with how to navigate in a multiplayer world.

The Importance of Help

The first command I run in any Minecraft multiplayer server is this:

```
/help
```

First of all, you never know which mods a particular server has installed, so the "vanilla" Minecraft console commands simply might not work. Second, some servers have strict behavior rules, and you run the risk of getting kicked or even banned from the server if you don't follow them.

Often a server's help menu spreads across multiple pages. For instance, issue the following command to see page 2:

```
/help 2
```

Cubeville's help system is shown in Figure 1.11.

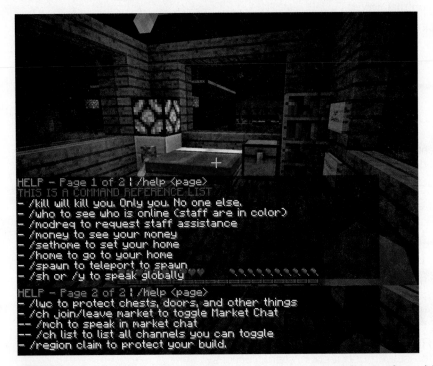

FIGURE 1.11   Running /help as soon as you enter a Minecraft multiplayer server is the best way to get your bearings and get the "lay of the land."

Chatting with OPs and Other Players

You can view a table of all currently connected players and server operators (OPs, pronounced "AHPs") by pressing and holding Tab, as shown in Figure 1.12.

Keep in mind that many Minecraft servers are modded and have their own custom commands; the default chat command is T. So if I wanted to say "Hello" to everyone on the server, I'd press T, type the following, and press Enter (or Return on Macs):

```
Hello!
```

Everyone else on the server would see

```
<PlayerID>Hello!
```

where `<PlayerID>` is your Minecraft username.

Let's say I wanted to send a private message to a user named zoey2010. I'd press slash (/) to open the console and type this:

```
/tell zoey2010 "Hi, Zoey!"
```

You can see the result on Zoey's screen in Figure 1.13.

FIGURE 1.12   Here we see all connected users. OPs are shown in an alternate color to make them easy to identify. The connection bars show how strong each user's connection to the server is.

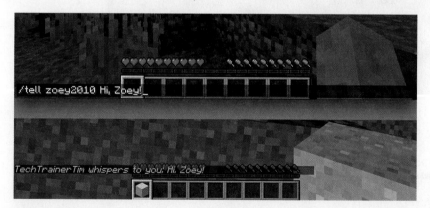

FIGURE 1.13   You use the /tell console command to send a private message to another player. The top image is from the sender's computer; the bottom image is from the receiver's computer.

Of course, you need to know the target player's ID in order to send a private message. Remember to press Tab (or try /list) to retrieve the player roster.

Setting Chat Options

The Minecraft client provides players a good degree of flexibility with regard to chat messages. From the Minecraft home page, click Options, Multiplayer Settings. The Chat Settings dialog is shown in Figure 1.14. Toggle the Chat button to suit your preference; the options are as listed here:

Shown: The default option; both chat and commands are shown onscreen.

Commands Only: Disables your ability to chat (you can send only console commands), but other users' chat activity still displays onscreen.

Hidden: Suppresses the entire chat screen.

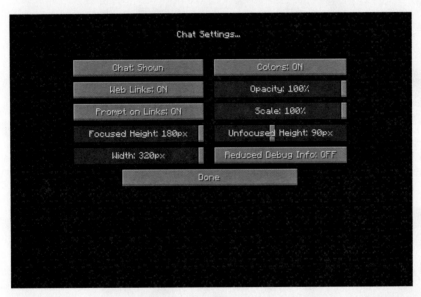

FIGURE 1.14 The Minecraft client gives players control over the appearance and verbosity of multiplayer chat messages.

> **NOTE**
>
> Minecraft Multiplayer is what's called a client/server application. In this context, your own personal copy of Minecraft is called the client. The server that you're connected to and playing on is called the server. Minecraft server operators are called OPs and have full permissions across the entire server.

In the name of completeness, let's describe the other chat settings:

Web Links: You can click hyperlinks that are posted to the chat pane.

Prompt on Links: You receive a confirmation before a clicked chat hyperlink works; this is a good security feature because you could infect your computer by clicking a malicious link.

Focused Height: The maximum height the chat pane is allowed to appear on your screen while you're using chat or commands.

Width: The maximum width of the chat pane.

Colors: Because I'm colorblind, I turn this off so all chat messages appear in a light gray color.

Opacity: The degree of transparency for the chat pane.

Scale: How large the chat pane appears on your screen.

Unfocused Height: The maximum height the chat pane is allowed to appear when you're not using chat or commands.

Show Cape: Whether vanity capes are shown on players' skins.

The Three Rules of Multiplayer Netiquette

I have three rules for general good Minecraft online multiplayer netiquette. If you follow these rules rigorously, you not only will be welcome at most Minecraft servers but might eventually be promoted to a moderator or administrator position based on your respect and courteousness.

Rule #1: Obey the Server Rules—Or Leave

Whether you're aware of it or not, by logging in to someone else's Minecraft multiplayer server, you agree to abide by any rules set forth by the server operator(s). If there's a "no griefing" rule, it's beyond silly for you to destroy another player's build or steal his property. It's true that some Minecraft server operators go a bit overboard with rules, but you don't have to stand for that. Simply find another server, or start your own and set the rules yourself!

Rule #2: Act in Accordance with the "Golden Rule"

The famous "Golden Rule" says, in effect, treat other players as you yourself would like to be treated. Would you enjoy another player on the server killing your Steve while you were hundreds of blocks away from your spawn? No, I didn't think so. Treat everybody on the server with respect, regardless of how they treat you. Again, if the situation is uncomfortable, disconnect from that server and find a nicer one.

Rule #3: Ask Without Fear

If you're wondering whether a particular behavior is allowed on a server, don't be afraid to ask an OP or another player. For me, the way that server staff and players treat me is a barometer for gauging how friendly a server's community is.

Of course, you should ask an OP questions only after you've thoroughly read the server rules.

The Bottom Line

I hope that you now have a better grasp of the player's experience of Minecraft multiplayer. You have the tools in your tool belt to identify high-value Minecraft servers, and you also understand how to configure your (legal) Minecraft launcher to connect to said servers.

In the next chapter we'll start our careers as Minecraft server operators. Specifically, we'll learn how to set up Mojang's own "vanilla" server on our local area network (LAN). See you there!

"Normal people...believe that if it ain't broke, don't fix it. Engineers believe that if it ain't broke, it doesn't have enough features yet."
—Scott Adams, *Dilbert* cartoonist

Building a Vanilla Minecraft Server

What You'll Learn in This Chapter:

- How the Java programming language relates to Minecraft
- How to install the vanilla server on Windows and OS X
- How to perform initial configuration tasks on the server
- Where to find vanilla online servers on the Internet

We'll get our hands dirty in this chapter by learning how to install and configure Mojang's own "vanilla" Minecraft server. Although chances are good that you'll go with another Minecraft server such as CraftBukkit to get maximum flexibility, it makes sense to start with the vanilla server because the underlying principles are all the same.

Without further ado, let's get to it!

Preparing the Java Environment

The Windows and OS X Minecraft versions are written in Java. Java, which in this context has absolutely nothing to do with the beverage, is a popular programming language that's used to write both desktop applications and web-browser-based apps.

To run a Java desktop application such as Minecraft, your Windows or OS X system needs to have the Java Runtime Environment (JRE) installed. We can look at the JRE as a sandbox that orchestrates the behavior of Minecraft client and Minecraft server.

As of this writing, the latest Minecraft release is version 1.8.2. The minimum JRE version supported by Minecraft is Java 6 Release 45.

TIP

Many people learn computer programming by writing Java modifications (called "mods") for Minecraft. If you'd like to try Java Minecraft programming, please check out the *Absolute Beginner's Guide to Minecraft Mods Programming* (ISBN 9780789753601), by my fellow Que Publishing author Rogers Cadenhead.

Verifying Your Java Version (Windows)

Perform the following steps on your Windows computer to make sure you have the JRE installed:

1 Press Windows+R to open the Run dialog box.

2 In the Run dialog box, type cmd and press Enter.

3 The Command Prompt window appears; type java -version and press Enter. If you have Java installed, you'll be given the specific build version, as shown in Figure 2.1. If you get an error, you don't have JRE installed and you should follow my instructions on downloading Java.

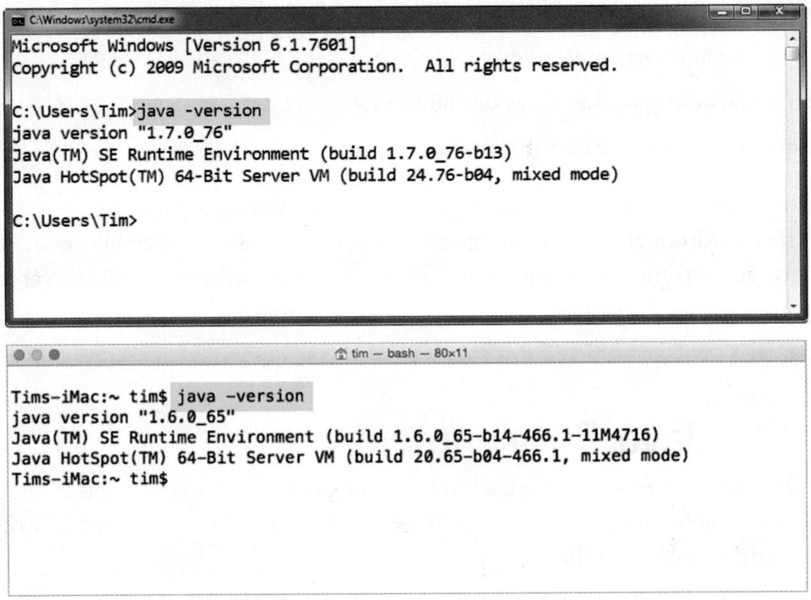

```
C:\Windows\system32\cmd.exe

Microsoft Windows [Version 6.1.7601]
Copyright (c) 2009 Microsoft Corporation.  All rights reserved.

C:\Users\Tim>java -version
java version "1.7.0_76"
Java(TM) SE Runtime Environment (build 1.7.0_76-b13)
Java HotSpot(TM) 64-Bit Server VM (build 24.76-b04, mixed mode)

C:\Users\Tim>
```

```
                          tim — bash — 80×11

Tims-iMac:~ tim$ java -version
java version "1.6.0_65"
Java(TM) SE Runtime Environment (build 1.6.0_65-b14-466.1-11M4716)
Java HotSpot(TM) 64-Bit Server VM (build 20.65-b04-466.1, mixed mode)
Tims-iMac:~ tim$
```

FIGURE 2.1 The top screenshot is from Windows 7, and the bottom screenshot is from OS X Yosemite. In both cases we verified that Java is installed and available.

Verifying Your Java Version (OS X)

Perform the following steps on your Mac computer to verify Java installation:

1 Press Cmd+spacebar to open the Search box.

2 In the Search box, type `terminal` and press Return.

3 The Terminal appears; type `java -version` and press Return. Make a note of your Java version (you can see an example in Figure 2.1). What's cool about OS X is that it always includes the JRE; this isn't the case with Microsoft Windows.

Downloading and Installing the JRE

If you don't have the JRE installed or are running an older version, point your web browser to http://www.java.com and download the latest version. The Java website detects your operating system version and offers you the appropriate installer.

One problem that Windows users might have is installing the JRE but getting an error message when running the `java -version` command. The first thing to do is to restart your computer and try again. If you still get a failure, follow this procedure to tell Windows where to find the Java program files:

1 Press Windows+R to bring up the Run dialog box.

2 In the Run box, type `control sysdm.cpl` and press Enter. In case you're wondering, `sysdm.cpl` is the actual filename of the Advanced System Properties Control Panel item.

3 In the Advanced System Properties dialog, navigate to the Advanced tab, and click Environment Variables.

4 In the Environment Variables dialog, scroll the System Variables list until you find Path. Select that line, and then click Edit.

5 In the Edit System Variable dialog, move the cursor to the end of the list; add a semicolon (;) but no spaces, and type/paste the path to the JRE program directory. On most systems the path should be

```
"C:\Program Files\Java\jre7\bin\java"
```

Because "Program Files" has a space, it's important that you enclose the previous file path in quotes. Also, if you're running JRE v6, you'll want to type `jre6`. The same goes for `jre8`.

I show you this workflow in Figure 2.2. Click OK to close all the dialog boxes. Open a new Command Prompt window and type `java -version` to ensure that the new PATH environment variable works properly.

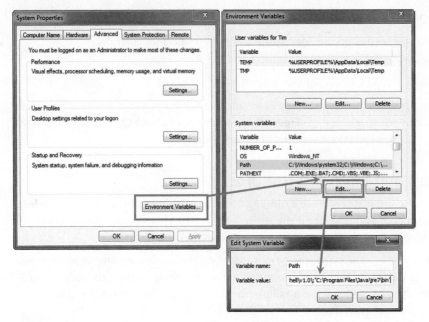

FIGURE 2.2 Adding Java to the Windows search path is a pain, but ultimately worth the trouble because Minecraft will actually work as expected.

Whew! Well, that was no fun. Personally, I hope that now that Microsoft owns Mojang they'll make setting up the Minecraft client environment more seamless than it is now. As a great YouTube sage once said, "Ain't nobody got time for that!"

Installing the Minecraft Server

Our goal in this chapter is to set up the Mojang-supplied Minecraft server. The Minecraft multiplayer community calls the Mojang server "vanilla" to indicate that this is a stable, but completely generic, Minecraft server.

What does this mean? The big news is that the vanilla Minecraft server is not modifiable. This fact is a deal-breaker for server administrators who want or need to add special functionality to their servers, for instance, anti-griefing tools or custom resources.

The main advantages that the vanilla server brings to the table are these:

- The vanilla server corresponds with the latest release of Minecraft client. This allows you to take advantage of all the latest game bug fixes and features.

- The vanilla server is supported by Mojang/Microsoft, and is far more stable than community Minecraft servers.

Don't panic—we're not going to put our new vanilla Minecraft server on the public Internet. No, no, no. What you'll be able to do is "stand up" a Minecraft server and log in to it anywhere on your private home network. I'm assuming that you're building this server on a home-based Windows or Mac computer that has shared Internet connectivity via Wi-Fi or wired Ethernet.

The Windows Installation Process

Before we dive into the step-by-step process, let me give you the high-level overview of what we're doing here:

- We'll put all our Minecraft server files in a single folder in an easy-to-find place on our computer's hard drive.
- We'll write a simple script to make it easier to start the Minecraft server.

Got it? Good—let's do this!

FOLLOW ME!
Install Minecraft Server on Windows

Perform the following steps to complete the procedure. If you're using a Mac, feel free to skip ahead to the section "The OS X Installation Process."

1 On your Windows computer, press Windows+R to open the Run dialog box.

2 In the Run box, type `c:` and then press Enter; a Windows File Explorer window appears.

3 Right-click in an empty area of the Windows File Explorer window and select New, Folder from the shortcut menu. Name the folder `mcserver`. Of course, you can use any name; the names I give you in the book are simply suggestions.

4 Pop open a web browser, navigate to Minecraft.net, and make sure you're logged in with your Mojang account. Next, click Download to access the Download page.

5 On the Download page, scroll to the Multiplayer Server section and download the `Minecraft_server.jar` file. This is important: Mojang makes available a Java Archive (`.jar`) version and a Windows Installer (`.exe`) version of the server. In my experience, it's far easier to use the native Java version.

6 Find the downloaded `.jar` file and move it to `C:\mcserver`. You know, come to think of it, you should configure Windows to show file extensions so that you can actually verify that you have the `.jar` file instead of the `.exe` one. I provide you with instructions on how to do that in the tip "How to Show File Extensions."

7 To make things even easier, we should rename the Minecraft server `.jar` file. Right-click the `.jar` file and select Rename from the shortcut menu. Name the file `minecraft-server.jar` and press Enter to confirm.

8 Now we'll create our startup script. Don't worry—you'll understand why we're doing this momentarily. For now, open Windows Notepad and save a file named `start.txt` in your `C:\mcserver` folder.

9 Add the following two lines of code to your new `start.txt` file. Make sure you have no extra spaces or strikes of the Enter key:

```
java -Xmx1024M -Xms1024M -jar minecraft-server.jar
pause
```

10 It's important that your `start.txt` script be located in the `C:\mcserver` folder along with the `minecraft-server.jar` file. Now close Notepad, saving your changes, and change the file extension of `start.txt` to `start.cmd`. You can do this, again, by right-clicking the file and selecting Rename from the shortcut menu. You'll be prompted to confirm the change. What we're doing in this step is making our text file an executable script file. Pretty cool, eh?

As a matter of fact, the file icon should have changed from a piece of notebook paper to a little window with gears on it, as shown in Figure 2.3. Looking at Figure 2.3 should serve as a nice "sanity check" for you to verify that you've completed all the steps correctly thus far.

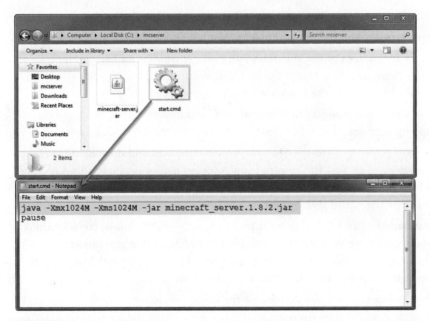

FIGURE 2.3   Our Windows-based vanilla Minecraft server installation environment.

TIP

How to Show File Extensions

By default, Windows hides file extensions, which are the three-character suffixes that identify what program is associated with particular files. As Minecraft server administrators, we need to configure our computer to show these extensions.

In Windows, open the Folder Options Control Panel, navigate to the View tab, and deselect the option Hide Extensions for Known File Types.

In OS X, click the Desktop background to select the Finder. Next, open the Finder menu and choose Preferences. In the Finder Preferences dialog box, enable the option Show All Filename Extensions. The Windows and Mac dialog boxes are shown in Figure 2.4.

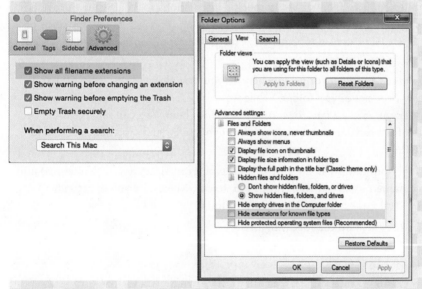

FIGURE 2.4 It's imperative that you configure your server to show all file extensions. OS X is at left; Windows is at right.

The OS X Installation Process

Please read through the Windows installation process so that you're familiar with our high-level goals. We'll now do the same steps, this time in an Apple environment.

FOLLOW ME!

Install Minecraft Server on OS X

Perform the following steps to complete the procedure. Even if you completed the installation on a Windows machine, you might learn a thing or two about Apple operating systems by working through these steps. I use OS X Yosemite, but the procedure should be the same for just about any OS X version.

1 From the Finder, open the Go menu and choose Home. We'll create our server folder inside our user's Home folder.

2 In the Home folder, right-click and select New Folder from the popup menu. Name the folder mcserver.

3 Open a web browser, navigate to minecraft.net, log in to your account, and download the Minecraft Server .jar file. I gave the specific instructions for that when I provided PC directions earlier in this chapter. If you haven't already done so, follow my steps in the "How to Show File Extensions" sidebar to reveal file extensions in Finder (this step will help you out a lot, I assure you).

4 Open your Downloads folder (or go to wherever you downloaded the .jar file) and move the file to your mcserver folder. While we're at it, rename the .jar file as minecraft-server.jar to cut down on misspellings later. You can rename a file by left-clicking the file's existing name once until it highlights, typing the new name, and pressing RETURN.

5 Open TextEdit (I normally press Cmd+spacebar, type textedit, and press Return) and save a new file named start in your mcserver folder. Make sure you're actually saving the file in your local mcserver folder and not iCloud!

6 In your new start file, add the following code:

```
#!/bin/bash
cd "$(dirname "$0")"
exec java -Xms1G -Xmx1G -jar minecraft-server.jar
```

You'll learn what those commands do in a moment; for now simply follow the steps! Close the file when you're finished editing it.

7 We need to change the file extension of our start file to tell the Mac that's it's actually an executable script file. Left-click the text file twice (slowly!), remove the original extension, and make it .command. OS X will prompt you to confirm the change; when you're finished, the file should be named start.command and have a funky icon. You can see all this in Figure 2.5.

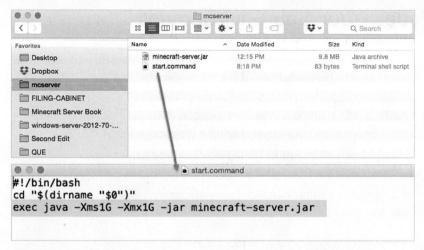

FIGURE 2.5 Our OS X–based vanilla Minecraft server installation environment.

8 We're almost finished. As nice as OS X is, after you get beneath the eye candy and down to the operating system's UNIX roots, things can get pretty complex quickly. In addition to changing the script's extension, we need to tell OS X directly that we want to execute this file instead of simply opening its source code.

To that end, in Finder click Go, Utilities, and then double-click the Terminal app.

9 Terminal should put you in your home folder. Issue the following command to change focus to your mcserver folder:

```
cd mcserver
```

10 In UNIX/Linux/OS X we use chmod (pronounced "C-H-mod" or "cha-MOD") to modify file permissions. Issue the following statement and press Return:

```
chmod a+x start.command
```

TIP

In my experience as a programmer, I find that most errors are the result of simply typographical screwups (affectionately called "typos"). I say this to give you confidence and avoid discouragement if you find that your Minecraft Server start scripts don't behave as initially expected. Take a close look at every letter and every character in the file—chances are that you typed an underscore instead of a hyphen, spelled "Minecraft" as "minecruft," or made a similar mistake.

An Interlude...Your Lab Environment

I want to say a few words about the Windows or Mac computer that you're using for this vanilla Minecraft server experiment. Although I trust that you verified that the box meets the Minecraft client system requirements, what about the server piece?

Here's a word to the wise: Random access memory, or RAM, is the hardware component with the greatest impact on Minecraft server performance. As more players log on to your server, gameplay will suffer terribly if your server doesn't have enough free RAM.

The good news is that right now we're just in testing mode, so you can use any computer that's less than, say, five years old with no problems.

As we'll learn in just a moment, it's best to give a Minecraft Server 1 gigabyte (GB) of RAM to play with when you have one to three players in a shared world.

Buy Another Copy of Minecraft? Really?

First of all, the $26.95 you pay to Mojang (I mean Microsoft; it's taking me a long time to get used to that fact now) doesn't give you any ownership of Minecraft the game. Instead, that money pays for a single-user license that grants you the right to *play* that game. Understand?

Second, I strongly suggest that you purchase a second Minecraft game license if you're serious about learning how to build and manage Minecraft servers. Why? It's very simple: How else can you test the operator (OP) and player experience if you don't have at least two valid players?

Now that those points have been discussed, let's get to the good stuff: firing up our new vanilla Minecraft server!

NOTE

The Origin of "Vanilla"

You should understand by now that the "vanilla" Minecraft server is the server that's offered by Mojang/Microsoft to its premium customers. The "vanilla" part means that this server cannot be modded or otherwise hacked like third-party server variants can. "What you see is what you get," in other words.

First Run and Initial Configuration Steps

The time has come to launch our vanilla Minecraft server! Go ahead and double-click `start.cmd` or `start.command`, depending on your operating system. Keep your `mcserver` folder open on your desktop as well, because you'll see a couple of things happen:

- The folder becomes populated with a folder and a couple of new files.

- The server stops in its tracks.

Don't be alarmed! This first-run behavior is totally normal. On my Mac, for instance, I saw the following message in a Terminal window:

```
You need to agree to the EULA in order to run the server. Go to
eula.txt for more info
```

You'll see the same message in your Windows Command Prompt window. As with any commercial computer software, you are bound by the restrictions in its end user license agreement, or EULA (pronounced "YOU-lah"). You can read the latest and greatest Minecraft server EULA on the Mojang website:

https://account.mojang.com/documents/minecraft_eula

Every Minecraft installation also includes a local eula.txt file. Double-click that `eula.txt` file to open the file in a text editor. The file is pretty sparse; locate the line

```
eula=false
```

and change `false` to `true`. Save and close the file. All done with that!

Understanding the Server Configuration Files

Let's start by revisiting the server startup script we created earlier. The main line of code in both the Windows and OS X versions is this:

```
java -Xmx1024M -Xms1024M -jar minecraft-server.jar
```

Here's what's going on:

- **java:** Calls the Java Runtime Environment (JRE) into action.

- **Xmx:** Specifies the maximum amount of RAM the Minecraft server can access.

- **Xms:** Specifies the initial amount of RAM given to the Minecraft server.

- **jar:** Points the JRE to a specific Java Archive (`jar`) file.

- **minecraft-server.jar:** The Minecraft server program file.

If you ever need to open your startup scripts for editing, right-click the file and choose Edit (Windows) or Open With (OS X). You'll be prompted to choose an editor—any text editor is fine. Don't use Microsoft Word or a full-fledged word processor because those programs tend to add unwanted extra data to our configuration files.

You'll note that Mojang recommends giving Minecraft server a static RAM allocation; in other words, the Xms and Xmx values are the same. This setting minimizes the work that the JRE needs to perform on behalf of Minecraft. For testing purposes, 1GB of RAM is sufficient. I would advise against lowering this value; if your server computer is that strapped for RAM, perhaps you should choose a different computer to host the server.

Now that we've accepted the EULA, go ahead and double-click the startup script again. You'll see more "action" in your mcserver folder, and you'll also see the Minecraft server console window as shown in Figure 2.6.

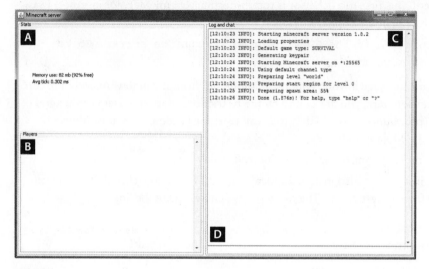

FIGURE 2.6   The vanilla Minecraft server console window. Here's a quick guide to what you see in Figure 2.6:

A: Displays how much RAM the server is consuming, along with the percentage of free RAM.

B: Lists players and OPs who are currently logged in to the server's world.

C: Presents detailed status messages and feedback from your OP console commands.

D: Allows you to issue console commands directly to the server.

Now take a look at Figure 2.7, which displays the contents of a fully populated mcserver folder. Following is a brief explanation of each asset in that folder.

FIGURE 2.7   These files compose a fully functional vanilla Minecraft server installation.

- **banned-ips.json:** Allows you to ban players by their computer's Internet Protocol (IP) address.

- **banned-players.json:** Allows you to ban players by their Minecraft username.

- **logs:** Folder that stores internal messages concerning the server.

- **ops.json:** Lists the user accounts with operator (OP) privilege on the server.

- **server.properties:** The main configuration file; enables you to customize the server's world.

- **usercache.json:** Reserves a memory/storage buffer for previously connected players to make their logons to your server faster.

- **whitelist.json:** Stores Minecraft usernames that are explicitly allowed to join the server's world.

- **world:** Folder that contains all the server's world assets.

NOTE

Do You Know JSON?

You'll observe that the vanilla Minecraft server uses the .json file extension to store its configuration data. JavaScript Object Notation, or JSON (pronounced "JAYS-on") is a simple, lightweight format for describing structured data. You can look at JSON files as mini-database files. What's cool about JSON configuration files is that you can edit them with any text editor, and the syntax is not cryptic.

The Minecraft Server Console

The best way to learn the Minecraft server console is to jump in and start playing with it.

FOLLOW ME!

Getting Comfortable with the Vanilla Minecraft Server

To complete the following steps, you should have your Minecraft server running and have the Minecraft client available on the same computer that runs the server.

1　We'll begin by asking Minecraft Server for command help. Type the following into the console (make sure to press Enter or Return after typing any console command):

```
/help
```

You should see a line of output that reads:

```
--- Showing help page 1 of 9 (/help <page>) ---
```

This means the server has eight more pages of help to show us. Go ahead and issue commands to view the subsequent help pages:

```
/help 2
/help 3
```

and so on.

In time you'll become very familiar with these server console commands.

2 Next we need to make sure that our Minecraft user has OP privileges on the server. Issue the following command to the server, substituting <username> with your Minecraft username:

```
/op <username>
```

Check the Log and Chat window for confirmation; on my machine it said "Opped TechTrainerTim." Note that the server will hit the Internet to verify the Minecraft username on Mojang.com. Therefore, I can't stress enough that you should be running a legal Minecraft instance!

3 Fire up your Minecraft client and start the game using the latest Minecraft version profile. From the home screen, click Multiplayer.

4 On the Play Multiplayer screen, click Direct Connect. You'll see the Direct Connect screen appear, as shown in Figure 2.8.

FIGURE 2.8 The Direct Connect screen.

5 We need to learn our computer's IP address in order to connect to the server. In Windows, open a command prompt window (you should know how to do that by now: Windows+R, Cmd, Enter), and type `ipconfig`. Look for an IP address that starts with `192.168`, `172.16`, or `10`.

On Macs, open a Terminal window (don't close the Terminal window launched by the Minecraft server!) and type `ifconfig | grep "inet "`. Again, look for an IP address in one of the numeric ranges I supplied. I show you the server IP addresses for my Mac and Windows computer in Figure 2.9.

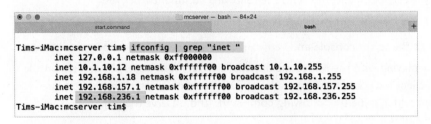

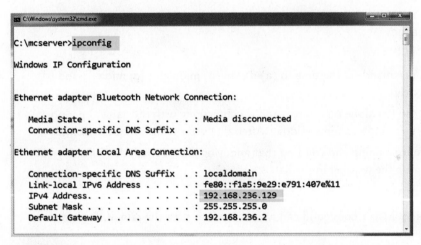

FIGURE 2.9   You need to know your server's IP address in order to connect to its shared world.

Frankly, if your computer has multiple IP addresses like mine does, you might need to try a couple of addresses in Minecraft before you find the correct one. And don't worry about that wacky `ifconfig` command I had you type on your Mac; we'll learn all the necessary networking information later in the book.

6 If you haven't already done so, type your computer's IP address in the Minecraft Play Multiplayer screen and press Enter/Return. You should be taken directly into the server's world.

7 Press Esc to pause the Minecraft client and return to the server. In the console, send a global broadcast message by using the /say command:

```
/say "Welcome to my server!"
```

8 Quickly switch back to your Minecraft client and verify that you see the server message. If you missed it, press T to open the chat pane. I show you what this looks like in Figure 2.10.

9 Because you're an OP, you can send a serverwide message from the client. Type a slash (/) to open the client console and send the following command:

```
/say "Hi from the Minecraft client!"
```

Switch back to the server console and verify that you see the message from your client.

10 Let's close by playing with the Minecraft day/night cycle. From either the server console or the game client (as you see, when you're an OP it doesn't matter where you issue console commands), issue the following commands and observe the in-game results:

```
/time set 0
/time set 18000
/time set 6000
/time set 12000
```

The previous command set the time to (a) dawn; (b) midnight; (c) midday; and (d) dusk, respectively.

Personally, when I'm alone on a server and experimenting with the game, I periodically issue /time set 6000 to force midday. After all, I want to see what I'm doing!

11 If the world starts raining and you find that annoying like I do, use the following command to clear up the weather immediately:

```
/toggledownfall
```

The /toggledownfall command can also be used to start the rain, if, for instance, your crops need some water.

Of course, Minecraft allows you to completely disable the day/night cycle if you're of the mind to do so:

```
/gamerule doDaylightCycle false
```

12 Keep your game session active, but go back to the server console and run the following command to stop the server:

```
/stop
```

You'll see the screen shown in Figure 2.11 in the Minecraft client as soon as the server goes offline.

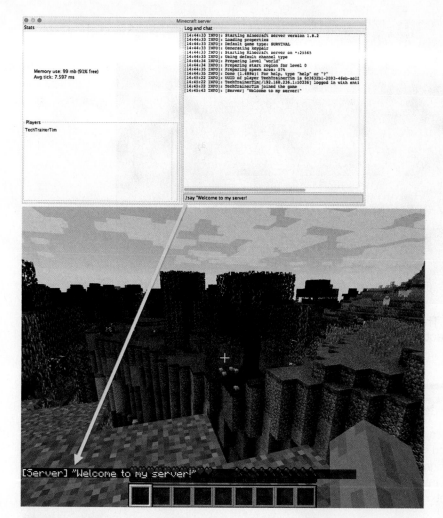

FIGURE 2.10 We send a server broadcast message from the server console (top), and then all connected players see the result (bottom).

FIGURE 2.11   This is what players see when the Minecraft server to which they're connected is shut down.

CAUTION

Don't forget to run /stop to formally shut down your Minecraft server instance when you're finished with it. By leaving the server up and running when you don't need it, you're (a) reducing the RAM available to your computer for other tasks; and (b) leaving your computer with an open door for unauthorized connection requests, even within your home network.

Running More Than One Server Instance

You can run multiple Minecraft server instances on the same computer. One reason why you'd do this is if you want to offer players different game modes. Each Minecraft server instance runs in its own protected memory space and is isolated from any other instance. Of course, you need to make sure that you have enough RAM on your computer to host more than one server instance. Believe me, after you begin ramping up the number of connected players, gameplay can get bogged down faster than you'd expect.

In a nutshell, here is what you need to do in order to have more than one vanilla Minecraft server on your computer:

- Set up two separate `mcserver` folders, assembling each as we've covered earlier in this chapter.

- Modify the listening port for each server.

Think of it this way: If your server has one IP address (let's say `192.168.1.2`) and two Minecraft servers, then how can players connect to serverA versus serverB—they both exist at the same IP address!

Long story short (see Chapter 4, "Understanding Networking as it Relates to Minecraft"), you'll want to add a unique server-port value in each instance's `server.properties` file.

Finding Vanilla Servers on the Internet

At this point you know how to bring a vanilla Minecraft server online in your own private network. Believe it or not, vanilla servers are actually in the minority on the Internet. The truth of the matter is that most Minecraft server administrators want or need the capability to mod the server to better suit their requirements and preferences.

Nonetheless, you can find online vanilla servers if you know where to look. For example, go to the Minecraft Forum PC Servers page (http://www.minecraftforum.net/forums/servers/pc-servers, shown in Figure 2.12) and run a forum search for "vanilla."

FIGURE 2.12 A section of the Minecraft Forum website is used to advertise Minecraft online servers, including ones of the vanilla variety.

One thing you'll notice about online vanilla servers is that they tend to be whitelisted. After all, vanilla server operators know they can't install mods to protect their worlds against griefing and malicious use.

The Bottom Line

If you worked through all the activities in this chapter, I heartily congratulate you. You're on the road to becoming a skilled Minecraft server administrator! The good news is that Minecraft server setup is not something that you need to mess around with every day.

We'll continue in the following chapter by learning how to perform day-to-day Minecraft server administration tasks. These are activities that you *will* be messing around with every day, so you'll want to give yourself plenty of practice time. See you then!

"In theory there is no difference between theory and practice. In practice there is."

–Yogi Berra

Operating a Vanilla Minecraft Server

What You'll Learn in This Chapter:

- Understanding our test environment
- Configuring your server's world
- Getting your users connected
- Interacting with your users
- Exerting discipline on your server
- Opening a single-player game to your LAN

This chapter is all about daily maintenance and management of a vanilla Minecraft server. In my experience, it makes the most sense to use the case study format as I teach you these new skills. If you're champing at the bit to use modded servers such as CraftBukkit, I gently remind you to be patient—we'll get to that shortly.

The good news is that you can apply all the skills you pick up in this chapter to any other Minecraft server environment. Let's begin.

Understanding Our Test Environment

Please spend a couple of minutes studying the Microsoft Visio drawing in Figure 3.1. The drawing shows how my home-based Minecraft server environment is set up.

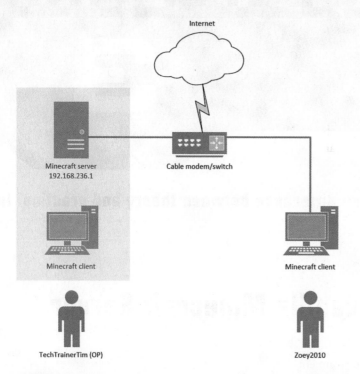

FIGURE 3.1 The vanilla Minecraft server environment we'll use for all examples in this chapter.

On the left in Figure 3.1 is my Apple iMac computer, which serves as both my Minecraft vanilla server and a Minecraft client for my TechTrainerTim OP account.

On the right is my Lenovo laptop that runs Windows 8.1 and the Minecraft client, this time logged on with my zoey2010 user account.

I mentioned in the preceding chapter that you should invest in two separate Minecraft user accounts so that you can practice your server administration skills in a safe "sandbox" environment. Trust me, your players will not come back to your server if you're "experimenting" on a server on which people spent a lot of time creating complex builds and such.

Finally, in the center of Figure 3.1 is my Comcast cable modem that connects my home network to the global Internet. In this chapter we're not concerned about Internet access because we're not ready to put our home vanilla server on the Net just yet. One step at a time.

Configuring the Server's World

If your Minecraft server is running, go to the console and issue the `/stop` command to bring it down. Next, open your `mcserver` folder and double-click `server.properties`. This is a simple plain-text file that you can edit in any basic text editor.

Introducing Sublime Text

I'm not receiving any kind of award or gift from the Sublime people for promoting their commercial text editor, Sublime Text (often affectionately called "Sublime" by devoted programmers).

You need to invest in a quality text editor if you plan to be an effective server administrator because most Minecraft configuration and customization involves the creation and editing of text files.

Professional programmers rely on Sublime Text. You can download the product free at the Sublime website (http://www.sublimetext.com), but a full per-user license costs $70. Yes, I know that's a steep price for some, but it's a good investment.

Figure 3.2 shows my customized `server.properties` as it appears in Sublime. The four annotations in that figure mark a few of my favorite features of this text editor:

A: You can open, edit, and save multiple files at once. In the figure, I have all my Minecraft server configuration files open in one window.

B: Sublime Text runs and behaves identically on Windows and OS X; this little widget in the corner is a thumbnail of the entire document. Thus, you can quickly navigate through long documents by using this control.

C: Sublime Text is totally customizable and scriptable in its own right. If you want to learn more about this, watch my friend Jesse Liberty's Pluralsight video training course "Sublime Text 3 from Scratch" (http://www.pluralsight.com/courses/sublime-text-3-from-scratch).

D: Sublime Text automatically determines the type of code you have in a file and performs syntax/keyword highlighting for you. Specifically, `server.properties` is a Java Properties file.

FIGURE 3.2   The customized `server.properties` file as rendered in Sublime Text.

Understanding `server.properties`

Because the `server.properties` file holds the master key to configuring your vanilla Minecraft server, I want to explain each and every option that's present in the in-box file.

The syntax of `server.properties` couldn't be easier; we simply have key/value pairs that are structured like this:

```
key=value
```

More properties exist than what Mojang gives you in the initial `server.properties` file; please research the Minecraft Wiki (http://minecraft.gamepedia.com/Server.properties) or another site to move your understanding to the next level.

Now I'd like to walk you through some of the more cogent `server.properties` settings:

- **spawn-protection:** Prevents non-OP players from placing or destroying blocks within a certain radius from their spawn point.

- **max-tick-time:** Determines how many milliseconds a game tick (time element) can take before the server is automatically shut down.

- **generator-settings:** Used to customize world generation.

- **force-gamemode:** If true, users must enter the server's default game mode (Creative, Survival, and so on). If false, the user will rejoin his or her last chosen game mode.

- **allow-nether:** If true, the world contains the Nether. If false, it doesn't.

- **gamemode:** Sets the worlds' default game type: 0 is Survival, 1 is Creative, 2 is Adventure, and 3 is Spectator.

- **enable-query:** True enables, and False disables, the ability for a GameSpy4 server to gather information about your server.

- **player-idle-timeout:** Number of minutes that a player can be idle before he or she is auto-kicked by your server.

- **difficulty:** 0 is Peaceful; 1 is Easy; 2 is Normal; 3 is Hard.

- **spawn-monsters:** If true, your world spawns hostile mobs after dark as usual.

- **op-permission-level:** 1 means that OPs can bypass spawn protection; 2 means that OPs can use /clear, /difficulty, /effect, /gamemode, /gamerule, /give, and /tp, and can edit command blocks.

- **resource-pack-hash:** Allows you to specify a verification digest for an installed resource pack; adding a value here supposedly improves resource caching on your server.

- **announce-player-achievements:** If true, the server allows all connected players to see the announcement whenever somebody earns an in-game achievement.

- **pvp:** If true, players can kill each other (PvP means "player versus player").

- **snooper-enabled:** If true, your server periodically sends usage data to Minecraft.net.

- **level-type:** The type of map that the server will generate. Options are DEFAULT, FLAT, LARGEBIOMES, AMPLIFIED, and CUSTOMIZED.

- **hardcore:** If true, players are banned from your server if they die.

- **enable-command-block:** If true, you can spawn and use command blocks in the world.

- **max-players:** The number of player slots on the server. Note that OPs cannot join a full server.

- **network-compression-threshold:** If set to 0, the server compresses its network traffic to save bandwidth and improve performance.

- **max-world-size:** Defines the world border as a block value.

- **server-port:** Specifies the TCP/IP port number that the Minecraft server listens on.

- **server-ip:** The Internet Protocol (IP) address on which your server listens for connection requests from players.

- **spawn-npcs:** If true, your world will spawn villagers (NPCs stands for "nonplayer characters").

- **allow-flight:** If true, players who have a flight mod installed may fly.

- **level-name:** The name of the world as it appears in-game and in your Minecraft server folder.

- **view-distance:** How much of the world the player sends to the client (measured in chunks in each direction from the player's position).

- **resource-pack:** Optional address to a resource pack.

- **spawn-animals:** If true, the server spawns animals as usual.

- **white-list:** If true, only players whose identities appear in whitelist.json are allowed to connect. OPs are always allowed to connect.

- **generate-structures:** If true, the server will generate villages, temples, and so on. Dungeons are always spawned.

- **online-mode:** If true, the Minecraft server verifies the players' accounts with Minecraft.net.

- **max-build-height:** The maximum height (y coordinate) that players are allowed to build.

- **level-seed:** Optionally specify a seed for your server's world. A *seed* is a globally unique alphanumeric string that represents the starting point and "address" of your world. Seeds can be shared among Minecrafters.

- **enable-rcon:** If true, you can access the Minecraft server console remotely.

- **motd:** The welcome/description message that appears below your server's name on the Play Multiplayer screen in the Minecraft client (MOTD stands for "Message of the Day").

After you've edited the server.properties file, save the changes and fire up your Minecraft server. *Note:* You'll need to stop and relaunch the server in order to make future server.properties changes take effect.

Getting Your User(s) Connected

By this point in your training, we're concerned only with our local area network (LAN). Therefore, the people who you want to join your server will need to bring their laptops over to your home and connect to your server's IP address.

Scanning, Scanning...

In a perfect world, your family and friends would do the following actions to join your Minecraft LAN server:

1 Start the Minecraft client.

2 Click Multiplayer.

3 See your LAN server in the Play Multiplayer screen.

4 Double-click the server to join the world.

However, as shown in Figure 3.3, you'll find in most cases that the Play Multiplayer screen perpetually says

    Scanning for games on your local network

FIGURE 3.3 I've had bad luck getting Minecraft LAN servers to show up in the Play Multiplayer screen (top). If you're lucky, though, you'll see the server's connection information appear (bottom).

The usual culprit here is that your players' computers and/or your Minecraft server have their local firewalls enabled. We won't get into the details here because we'll cover firewalls and connectivity troubleshooting in Chapter 4, "Understanding Networking as it Relates to Minecraft."

For now, you should switch to your Minecraft server console, scroll back in the Log output, and look for a line that looks like the following:

```
Starting Minecraft server on 192.168.1.18:25565
```

Of course, you'll probably have a different IP address, but the effect is the same: You need to share your LAN server's IP address with your players and instruct them to (a) click Add Server in the Play Multiplayer screen and (b) enter that IP address, as shown in Figure 3.4.

Minecraft uses port 25565 by default, but knowing port numbers is necessary only when you're hosting more than one multiplayer world on the same server.

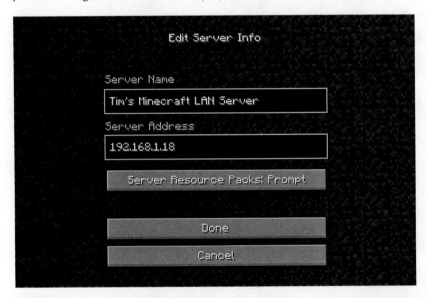

FIGURE 3.4 In my experience, sharing my server's IP address with local players is the fastest way to get them into the game.

TIP

One of my goals is to get you into the habit of reading (and understanding) your Minecraft server logs. Good systems administrators regularly scan logfiles to learn exactly what the server is doing (or not doing) on a daily basis.

Interacting with Your Users

As a Minecraft vanilla server operator, you'll find that the Minecraft server console is your best friend. The Minecraft server console user interface (UI) has four elements, as shown in Figure 3.5:

- **Stats:** Shows you how much RAM the server is consuming and the average tick speed in milliseconds (lower values are better here).

- **Players:** This is a read-only list, but it's helpful to know who is logged in to your server!

- **Log and chat:** This is the "meat and potatoes" of the interface. Minecraft logs everything that happens on the server here.

- **Console prompt:** You can type server commands here (always prefix commands with a slash) or in the Minecraft client.

FIGURE 3.5 The Minecraft server console gives you full command and control over your multiplayer world.

Speaking of logs, don't feel pressure to memorize every log entry in the Minecraft server console. Minecraft writes its log entries to files. Go to your `mcserver` folder and navigate to the `logs` subfolder. The current log is named `latest.log` and can be opened in Sublime Text or any other text editor. The compressed archive files can be extracted with a double left-click (see Figure 3.6).

Whenever a user connects to the server, you'll see two lines of output that look like this:

```
[09:56:49 INFO]: UUID of player zoey2010 is e0579eaf-f9c1-4685-9487-
b0b16f2c04fe
[09:56:49 INFO]: zoey2010[/192.168.1.15:52485] logged in
➥with entity id 313 at (-1.8216737492521475, 64.0,
➥123.33218141889492)
```

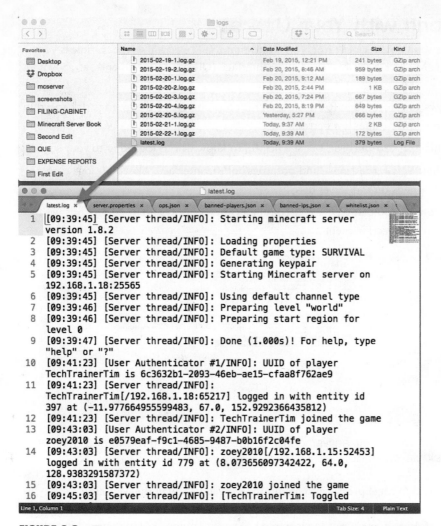

FIGURE 3.6 The conscientious server administrator, for Minecraft or other platforms, regularly scans log files for errors and other useful data.

The first line identifies the player's universally unique identifier (UUID), which is a long hexadecimal string that uniquely identifies the entity across the entire Mojang/Microsoft ecosystem. In fact, you can visit websites such as mcuuid.net (shown in Figure 3.7) to resolve a UUID to a username, and vice versa. This information can be helpful in troubleshooting.

Let's cut to the chase and learn how to interact with our players!

FIGURE 3.7 Every registered Minecraft player has a UUID (as does every asset in the game, such as mobs, trees, and blocks).

/say, /tell, and /me

By default, your users can broadcast chat messages by pressing T, typing their message, and pressing Enter or Return (see Figure 3.8).

By contrast, /say is available only to operators (OPs). If zoey2010, my regular player, tries to do something like

```
/say Is this thing on?
```

the console will tell her this:

```
You do not have permission to use this command
```

When the OP uses /say, the console will respond like this:

```
/say This is the OP speaking
```

FIGURE 3.8 Most Minecraft multiplayer players get the hang of using the chat key (the default is T) to send serverwide messages.

TIP

The Minecraft Wiki has a comprehensive list of Minecraft multiplayer console commands:

http://minecraft.gamepedia.com/Commands

The chat message shows up on all players' sessions, but the OP's username is enclosed in square brackets instead of angle brackets, like so:

```
[op-playername]
<regularuser-playername>
```

As shown in Figure 3.9, you should instruct your players to use Tab to show the player list. This is useful because you need to know somebody's player name before you can send the person a private chat message.

FIGURE 3.9   This screenshot is a mashup that shows the results of pressing Tab (player list, shown at top) and T (chat history, shown at bottom).

TIP

Clearing the Chat Window

For a color-blind person like me, I often get lost and confused when I visit an online server that's heavily populated and where lots of chat is going on. As a vanilla OP you can (theoretically) clear the chat window by using command blocks (here's a nice YouTube tutorial that covers this: https://www.youtube.com/watch?v=-RcXppuOrrk). However, using another Minecraft server along with plugins gives you a much cleaner experience. More will be revealed later in the book, I promise!

Speaking of sending private chat messages, that's what /tell is for. Here's the syntax:

```
/tell <targetplayername> your_message
```

So if I want to send zoey2010 a message, I can do the following:

```
/te[3 Tabs] z[Tab] Hey, Zoey! Welcome to my server.
```

So what's the Tab business all about? You *need* to take advantage of autocomplete in the Minecraft console. When you press the Tab key, Minecraft attempts to complete the rest of the command, parameter, or value that you want to execute.

For example, typing /t and then repeatedly pressing Tab cycles you through all the console commands that begin with "t." As you can see in Figure 3.10, the console even lists the possible matches for you.

When you've found the correct command, simply start to type the next element. For /tell, that would be the player's username. Again, Minecraft helpfully attempts to autocomplete player names. Of course, you'll see only entries for active users on your server.

FIGURE 3.10 If you're not taking advantage of command autocompletion in the Minecraft client, you should be.

Finally, we use /me (players and OPs) to relay the status to the rest of the server's population. For example, zoey2010 might type this:

```
/me looking for a place to build my house
```

Status update messages show up in the chat window with an "x" prefix, as shown in Figure 3.11.

FIGURE 3.11 We use /me as a way of broadcasting our status on the server (this is Minecraft multiplayer's version of the Twitter or Facebook status update).

/tp and /give

Let's say that zoey2010 finds herself lost and sends the OP (TechTrainerTim, our other account) a private message saying the following:

```
/tell TechTrainerTim Help! I'm lost and don't have any supplies!
```

We can use the /tp (teleport) OP command to teleport to Zoey's location. Here's the general command syntax:

```
/tp <teleporting-playername> <targetplayer>
```

If you know the Minecraft coordinates to where you want to go, you can teleport yourself or another player to that location:

```
/tp zoey2010 -3 64 106
```

Remember that in the Minecraft coordinate system the first number (x) refers to your distance east (positive) or west (negative) of the world's origin. The second number (y) refers to your player's elevation, with 64 being sea level. Finally, the third number (z) refers to your distance south (positive) or north (negative) of the world's origin.

A player can retrieve his or her location coordinates by invoking the debug window through keyboard shortcuts. Here they are for Windows and Mac; note that this is a toggle switch (in other words, you need to use the same keyboard shortcut to turn off debug mode):

Windows: F3, Fn+F3, or Fn+Alt+F3 (depending on your keyboard)

OS X: Fn+Alt+F3

As kind and beneficent OPs, we can pull any Minecraft game item out of thin air and equip it to any player on our server. Here's the general syntax:

```
/give <target-player> <item> <amount>
```

You have to know the item id or block id of the asset that you want to give. Check out Minecraftopia (http://www.minecraftopia.com/minecraft_ids) or a similar site to quickly look up these values.

The good news is that the Minecraft client's auto-complete also works great for quickly resolving Minecraft object IDs (Refer back to Figure 3.10).

In this example, let's give zoey2010 64 diamonds:

```
/give zoey2010 minecraft:diamond 64
```

We must really like zoey2010, right?

Exerting Discipline on Your Server

I've used the term "griefing" a bit in this book, but I've found that you don't appreciate what a hassle griefers can give you until you're managing a server and they actually begin causing damage.

I feel extraordinarily guilty and responsible if one of my players loses hours of construction work due to a few TNT blasts from a griefing player. Or perhaps a trusting player leaves a chest full of hard-earned diamonds in her base, only to have it mercilessly plundered by a griefer.

NOTE

The term "griefing" didn't originate with Minecraft. The word comes from the noun *grief*, which means deep sorrow, trouble, or annoyance. Thus, to "grief" another Minecraft player is to cause grief not only to the affected player, but to the OP as well.

Griefing makes players and OPs angry. In fact, one of the biggest weaknesses of the vanilla Minecraft server is the lack of built-in antigriefing tools.

Nonetheless, we have some native console commands that you'll use a lot to manage unruly players.

/kick

The /kick command is the mildest form of discipline, outside of sending the player a warning /tell message. Specifically, this command forcibly disconnects the user. Here's the syntax:

```
/kick <playername> <optional-reason>
```

Let's turn the tables and kick zoey2010 for experimentation purposes:

```
/kick zoey2010 I warned you, but you refuse to follow the rules.
```

Adding a reason to your /kick command is optional, but I suggest doing so because you might educate the player into behaving better the next time he or she connects to your server. Figure 3.12 shows what a kick looks like from the player's perspective.

The player won't lose his or her inventory if you allow the player to reenter the world.

FIGURE 3.12 This is what a kicked player sees: either the default message (top) or an OP-provided custom reason.

The trouble with /kick is that nothing prevents the user from simply reconnecting to your server. To wield a heavier hammer, we must turn to /ban or /ban-ip.

/ban and /ban-ip

A ban is a much harsher punishment, and should be reserved only for those players who simply refuse to follow the rules no matter how many times you warn and/or kick them. Here's the syntax:

```
/ban <player-name> <optional reason>
```

Again, the reason parameter is optional but definitely a good idea so that you at least attempt to maintain solid communication with the player. Let's ban zoey2010:

```
/ban zoey2010 This ban is only for testing purposes; don't sweat it!
:)
```

Upon reconnect, a user will see the error message shown in Figure 3.13 and he'll be prevented from logging in to your server.

Figure 3.14 shows you what the player sees if she tries to reconnect to your server while under a ban.

FIGURE 3.13 What the player sees in the Minecraft client if he tries to connect to your server by using a banned account.

FIGURE 3.14 What the player sees if she tries to connect to a server that banned her.

Sometimes sneaky players who have more than one registered Minecraft account will try to "back door" their way into your server. As long as the banned player is attempting multiple connections from the same IP address, we can put a ban on the address itself. The general syntax is as follows:

```
/ban-ip <ip-address> <optional-reason)
```

Check your server console or a server log file to determine the user's IP address. For example, here's the entry for the player zoey2010:

```
[11:31:20 INFO]: zoey2010[/192.168.1.15:52673] logged in
➥with entity id 20980 at (-29.69999998807907, 63.0,
➥104.68999142434426)
```

Now for the ban:

```
/ban-ip 192.168.1.15
```

The player's view of his IP address ban is shown in Figure 3.15.

FIGURE 3.15 What the player sees if your server has banned his computer's IP address.

/pardon, /pardon-ip, and /whitelist

The /pardon and /pardon-ip commands are the opposites of the /ban and /ban-ip commands. Now that we have the general command syntax down, let's go ahead and unban both zoey2010's IP address and her user account:

```
/pardon-ip 192.168.1.15
/pardon zoey2010
```

The whitelist is the list of approved Minecraft players. Note that OPs can always connect to the server, even if their names aren't in the whitelist.

First, we'll add zoey2010 to our whitelist:

```
/whitelist add zoey2010
```

Second, we'll verify that she's in there:

```
/whitelist list
```

Third, we'll turn on the whitelist:

```
/whitelist on
```

Remember that Minecraft server stores its metadata in various configuration files. The whitelist.json file contains the username and UUID of all whitelisted players; my file contents are shown in Figure 3.16.

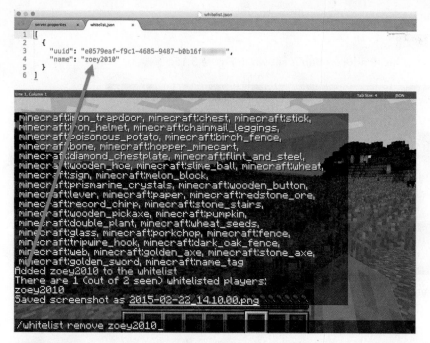

FIGURE 3.16 You can edit `whitelist.json` directly if you want to (top), or you can use the `/whitelist` console commands from the server console or in the client (bottom).

Let's remove zoey2010 from the whitelist:

```
/whitelist remove zoey2010
```

What would be interesting now is to see what happens when Zoey, whose account no longer exists in the whitelist, attempts to connect. The results are as expected and as shown in Figure 3.17—no connection to a whitelist server.

FIGURE 3.17 Players whose names aren't included in the whitelist are prevented from logging in to the whitelist server; this is perfectly expected behavior.

To complete this exercise, we'll turn off the whitelist:

```
/whitelist off
```

Adding a Management Layer to Your Server

The main reason I began using Minecraft server management "front ends" is because I needed an easier way to take backups. It makes my blood run cold to think of my Minecraft server crashing and potentially losing my players' progress and world builds. That's an awful thought, for sure.

With vanilla Minecraft we can, of course, manually copy our `mcserver` folder to an external hard drive, cloud storage service such as Dropbox, or the like. However, utilities exist to automate this backup process and make partial or full world restore possible as well.

Introducing McMyAdmin

Minecraft management front ends (also called "wrappers") are programs that surround, or wrap, the Minecraft server jar and give you an easier interface for administering your Minecraft server. You can check the Minecraft Wiki for a comprehensive list of wrappers (http://minecraft.gamepedia.com/Programs_and_editors/Server_wrappers), but here we'll focus on my favorite, McMyAdmin (http://www.mcmyadmin.com).

Take a look at Figure 3.18, which shows McMyAdmin in action.

FIGURE 3.18 McMyAdmin simplifies your life as a Minecraft server administrator.

Isn't that awesome? McMyAdmin is a web-based Minecraft management portal that you can use both for your local LAN servers and for those you rent from Minecraft server providers. Because McMyAdmin works not only with providers but also with third-party servers such as Bukkit, we'll use McMyAdmin quite a bit throughout the rest of this book.

FOLLOW ME!

Install McMyAdmin Under Windows

In this exercise you'll learn how to install McMyAdmin on your Windows computer to manage a local vanilla Minecraft server instance. McMyAdmin on OS X is a bit more complex and very poorly documented; search the Web for further guidance.

If you have another Minecraft server running on your computer, go ahead and issue the /stop command to stop it. You can leave your Minecraft client open if you want.

1 Go to the McMyAdmin website at mcmyadmin.com and download the latest version of the software. You'll see the download link on the home page.

2 Find MCMA2_Installer.exe in your Downloads folder and double-click to start the McMyAdmin installation routine.

3 Proceed through the installer by (a) accepting the EULA; (b) passing the built-in system checks; (c) specifying an installation path (I chose my home folder); (d) supplying a strong password to protect the console; and (e) specifying system settings such as port number, IP address, and whether you want to run the software as a service (I choose to do so).

4 When the installer finishes, click OK. Your default web browser starts, and the McMyAdmin logon screen appears as shown in Figure 3.19. The default username is admin, and the password is what you specified during the McMyAdmin installation.

FIGURE 3.19 The McMyAdmin logon screen.

Installation Notes

The most common installation errors are missing prerequisites. Make sure that you have the Java Runtime Environment (JRE) installed; get the software from http://www.java.com.

McMyAdmin also requires the Microsoft .NET Framework 3.5. You should already have this .NET version installed if you run a relatively recent version of Windows (such as Windows 7 or Windows 8.1). However, you can download .NET Framework 3.5 directly from Microsoft: https://www.microsoft.com/en-us/download/details.aspx?id=21. Make sure to run Microsoft Update from the Control Panel after you install to pick up any bug fixes to this (old) version of the .NET Framework.

Configuration Notes

McMyAdmin downloads and uses its own personal copy of the vanilla Minecraft server. So forget about any vanilla servers that you've installed separately. This means, of course, that you'll need to redo your `server.properties` settings.

In the McMyAdmin console, navigate to the Configuration node and work through setting options here. It's a much easier and simpler-to-comprehend interface, right?.

When you're ready to start the McMyAdmin server, navigate to Status and click Start Server. McMyAdmin takes care of the EULA acceptance for you automatically.

Finally, navigate to the Console node if you want to issue console commands, and hit up the Backups node (shown in Figure 3.20) to manage world backup and restore. Now this is Minecraft server administration!

FIGURE 3.20 McMyAdmin makes it easy to back up and restore your shared Minecraft worlds.

McMyAdmin Editions

McMyAdmin Personal Edition, which we use here by installing the software without a license key, has some limitations that you should be aware of. The chief limitation is that you can host a maximum of ten players in-game. This should be fine for home-based LAN games, but isn't sufficient for an Internet-based server that hopefully will host dozens of users.

If you love McMyAdmin, you might want to consider investing $15.40 USD (as of this writing in spring 2015) in the Professional Edition, which has no in-game user limit. View a McMyAdmin edition comparison matrix at their website: https://www.mcmyadmin.com/#/editions.

Opening a Single-Player Game to the LAN

I want to finish this chapter by speaking briefly about the Minecraft client's built-in server. Did you know that you can open your single-player game to LAN multiplayer? Yes indeed. Here's the procedure:

FOLLOW ME!

Opening Up a Single-Player Game to Multiplayer

In this exercise we'll start a single-player game and then turn it into a LAN-based multiplayer game. Please stop any server instances that you have running. You can stop your McMyAdmin server instance by switching to the web GUI, navigating to the Status page, and clicking Stop Server.

1 Go to the home page of the Minecraft client and click Singleplayer.

2 Click Create New World. Name the world "My Shared World," customize the world options to your liking, and then click Create New World.

3 After you're in the world, press Esc to invoke the game menu. Next, click Open to LAN, as shown in Figure 3.21.

4 In the LAN World dialog, shown in Figure 3.22, choose the game mode and whether you'll allow console commands. Next, click Start LAN World.

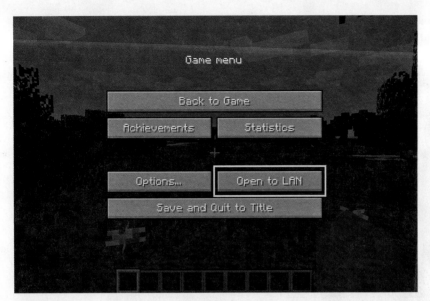

FIGURE 3.21 Many Minecraft players never even notice the Open to LAN button.

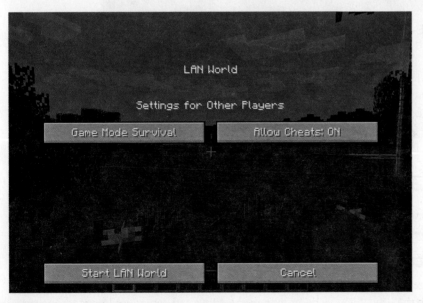

FIGURE 3.22 You have limited administrative control over a single-player game that you "publish" to your local area network (LAN).

5 On another computer, start the Minecraft client, click Multiplayer, and double-click the shared world that should appear in the Play Multiplayer list (Figure 3.23).

FIGURE 3.23   Barring firewall and network connectivity issues, your players should be able to see your shared server on your local network.

If the shared server doesn't show up, click Add Server and type the connection information of the hosting server. For example, my server's IP address is 192.168.1.18, and my chat console says this:

```
Local game hosted on port 55089
```

Therefore, we can use the following as our connection string in the Edit Server Info dialog box:

```
192.168.1.18:55089
```

6 Your connected users will automatically be kicked after you quit the shared LAN game.

The Bottom Line

If you've managed Minecraft servers in the past, I hope you have picked up some new tips and tricks along the way. If you've never managed a Minecraft server until now, I hope this has helped to get you started on the right foot. If you're an inquisitive sort like I am, you probably want to know more about "under the hood" details such as IP addresses, port numbers, firewalls, and the like. Having a basic knowledge of computer networking is crucial to protecting your Minecraft server (especially Internet-facing ones) from attack.

To that point, in the next chapter we'll spend time learning all the basics of networking and applying those skills to a Minecraft server.

4

"Fools ignore complexity. Pragmatists suffer it. Some can avoid it. Geniuses remove it."

–Alan Perlis, American computer scientist and first recipient of the Turing Award

Understanding Networking as It Relates to Minecraft

What You'll Learn in This Chapter:

- How TCP/IP networking relates to Minecraft multiplayer
- How to view your computer and router IP settings
- How to put your home-based Minecraft server on the Internet
- How to use a friendly hostname for your server instead of an unfriendly IP address

I'm not sure if you're aware of it, but Minecraft is being used all over the world, every day, as an educational tool. Gaming as a teaching and learning method isn't exactly new; however, Minecraft is such a rich and varied game that you can approach not only gameplay, but the game itself in many different directions.

One of my goals in writing this book is to generate interest in my readers, especially my younger readers, in systems administration. The IT field has been spectacular to me since I entered it in 1997, and there's room for you too!

If you're interested in discovering the magic of computer programming, developing Minecraft mods might be just the ticket to get you started. In this chapter we cover computer networking (a huge topic) in the space of only a couple dozen pages.

By the end of the chapter, you not only will understand what you need to do to put your Minecraft LAN server on the public Internet to host external players, but also will know the "hows" and "whys" behind your configuration. And who knows—you might discover that you have enough passion and aptitude for server administration that you might want to make a career of it!

Let's begin!

Revisiting Our Test Network

I want to share another network diagram with you that shows the topology we'll be working with. "Topology" is a networking term that simply refers to the physical arrangement of computers and associated devices on a single network.

You can see the topology in Figure 4.1. Let me describe the major working parts:

- Workpc1 is a Windows 8.1 desktop computer that hosts a vanilla Minecraft server. The computer receives its IP address from the cable modem.

- Win8 is a Windows 8.1 laptop computer that, like Workpc1, obtains its IP address from the cable modem.

- The cable modem is directly connected to the Internet. The device has an Internet-connected IP address and an internal, private interface that connects to Workpc1 and Win8. The router (because that's actually what the cable "modem" is) performs Network Address Translation (NAT) and Dynamic Host Configuration Protocol (DHCP) services on behalf of Workpc1 and Win8.

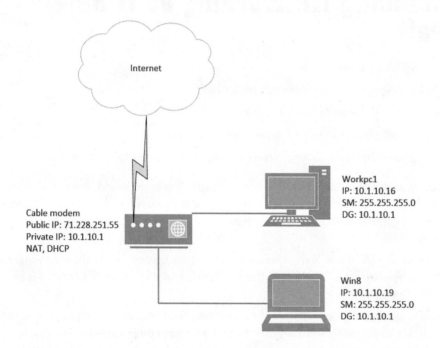

FIGURE 4.1 The home-based network that we'll use as a case study in this chapter.

Learning as We Go: Basic Networking Terminology

Rather than give you dry, boring explanations of the basic networking vocabulary terms, we'll simply use the terms in context as we work with our network devices.

You'll notice that I use the term *network devices* (or hosts) instead of *computers*. I do this because on a TCP/IP network, any electronic device that has a network interface card (NIC) installed is considered a node, or device, on that network. By this definition, any of the following pieces of hardware can be considered to be network hosts:

- Laptop computer
- Smartphone
- Tablet (iPad, Microsoft Surface, and so on)
- Wi-Fi router
- Smart TV
- Raspberry Pi
- Smart watch

TCP/IP stands for Transmission Control Protocol/Internet Protocol, and it describes a whole bunch of networking protocols, of which TCP and IP are only two. TCP/IP has been the standard networking protocol in the world for the past 20 years or so.

IP Addresses

For our purposes as Minecraft server administrators, the Internet Protocol (IP) address is the most important concept to master. A networking protocol, such as IP, is simply a set of rules that a TCP/IP host uses to communicate with another host. The sending and receiving of data, in other words.

Specifically, a host's IP address serves to uniquely identify that device on its network. In Figure 4.1, for instance, the cable modem has the IP address 10.1.10.1, Workpc1 has 10.1.10.16, and Win8 has 10.1.10.19.

How do we know that these IP addresses exist on the same network? Besides the fact that the devices are all physically (or wirelessly) connected to the cable modem router, we can take a look at their subnet mask.

The subnet mask is a combination of decimal 255s and 0s that separates the network portion of the address from the host (device) portion. Look at Figure 4.2 to illustrate.

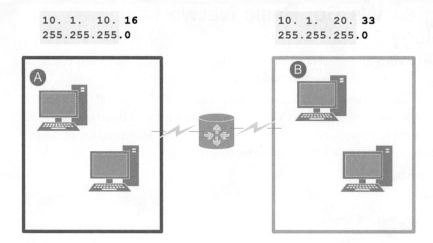

FIGURE 4.2 TCP/IP hosts use their subnet mask to differentiate their network address as well as host ID.

In Figure 4.2, we have computer A, with IP address `10.1.10.16`, attempting to exchange data with computer B, with IP address `10.1.20.33`. Computer A "examines" its subnet mask, which "covers" up three of the four parts of an IP address, and determines that `10.1.10` is its own network. Because the target IP address is on network `10.1.20`, computer A "decides" it needs to send its traffic to its default gateway (router). The purpose of the router is to serve as a "traffic director" between different IP networks.

To be frank, we don't need to worry about subnet masks too much for what we're doing; I just want to make sure that you have a well-rounded understanding.

Private and Public Addresses

Let's return to Figure 4.1. If we install Minecraft server on Workpc1, we should have no trouble connecting to the game from Workpc1 because, as we already discussed, the two computers have the same IP network address.

I'll go so far as to say that if our cable modem had another interface connected to a network address of, say, `10.1.20`, then those computers still could connect to our game.

However, if our friend from across town (or on the other side of the world) tries to connect to your Minecraft server with a `10.` IP address, then he or she will never connect. Not ever. What's going on?

It's a long story, but suffice it to say that the world has run short of public IP addresses that are visible across the Internet. Because of this shortage, routers/cable modems/wireless access points use private IP addresses and two more protocols to bridge the gap.

First, about private IP addresses: You might have noticed that whenever you connect to somebody's Wi-Fi network you receive an IP address from one of the following ranges:

- `10.0.0.0-10.255.255.255`
- `172.16.0.0-172.32.255.255`
- `192.168.0.0-192.168.255.255`

Those IP addresses are called private network addresses because the world has agreed never to route them. You simply cannot send or receive data across the Internet by using a private IP address. Remember what I said about the shortage of public IP addresses; private addresses were developed as a workaround.

Network Address Translation

You're probably wondering, "If my computer can't communicate on the Internet with a private IP address, then how the heck am I able to surf the Web in the first place?!" The answer is one of those "two additional protocols" I mentioned that your cable modem has: Network Address Translation, or NAT (pronounced like the tiny flying insect).

Your cable modem (or whatever device you use to access the public Internet) has only one public IP address. That's all you get from your Internet service provider (ISP). When I started in IT back in 1997, all computers received public IP addresses from their ISP; those days are long gone now.

With NAT, a router can "share" a single public IP address with more than one device on the internal network. Do you see the beauty here? We can have as many devices inside our network as we want because we're using private IP addressing. All devices connect to the router, and the router serves as a proxy, or go-between, for the Internet and your internal devices.

Of course, some of you are now likely wondering, "How do my internal devices get their private IP addresses? Do they come from the router, my ISP, both, or neither?" That's actually a great question.

DHCP

Dynamic Host Configuration Protocol (DHCP) is a service for dispensing and managing a range of IP addresses to one or more client devices. It's standard nowadays for your router to serve as a DHCP server. In fact, most routers enable you to edit how DHCP behaves by allowing you to log in to the router directly.

Let's now apply our newfound networking know-how to what's really important: making our Minecraft server available to players from all over the world!

Taking the Next Step: Preparing Our Network for Minecraft Server

I need to issue a word of warning, especially if you're following along with these procedures in your home network environment. Advertising a vanilla Minecraft server to the Internet from home isn't something you want to do long-term. The reason for this centers on privacy—you likely have more than just Minecraft data on that box. Do you really want to allow anonymous connections from all over the world into your home network and home computer? I didn't think so.

Sure, for testing and learning the technology it's fine, but if you want to do anything more than host a few close friends for some Minecraft fun, then I suggest that you consider not only using an honest-to-goodness Minecraft host, but also using a third-party server instead of the vanilla one.

I already mentioned the security and privacy issue as a "deal breaker" for most home-based Minecraft installations. As you work through the rest of this book I'll make an excellent case for using an online hosting service—be patient!

Discovering Our Computer's Networking Configuration

You can quickly and easily find out what your computer's TCP/IP configuration is either by using graphical tools built directly into the operating system, or by using command-line tools. I'll focus on GUI tools so that we can spend more time analyzing the data and less horsing around with command-line arguments.

On Windows computers, follow this procedure:

1 Press Windows+R to bring up the Run dialog box.

2 Type ncpa.cpl and press Enter. This command opens your network connections folder and in my experience is much faster than monkeying around with Control Panel.

3 In the Network Connections folder, double-click the appropriate network interface.

4 In the Ethernet Status window, click Details.

5 In the Network Connection Details window, shown in Figure 4.3, scan the output, paying attention to the following fields:

IPv4 Address

IPv4 Subnet Mask

IPv4 Default Gateway (this is the router's internal IP address)

IPv4 DHCP Server (this should also point to your router's internal IP address)

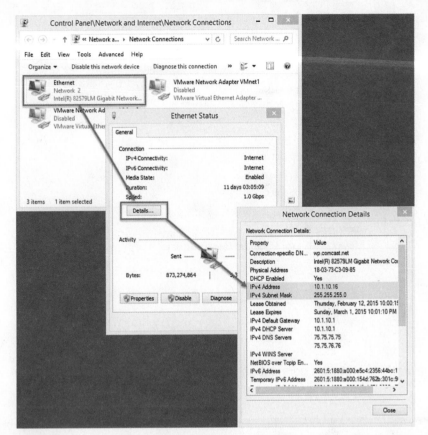

FIGURE 4.3 The Windows Control Panel gives us access to all computer TCP/IP configuration settings.

On OS X computers, try the following:

1 Open the Apple menu and click System Preferences.

2 In the System Preferences pane, click Network.

3 In the Network window, shown in Figure 4.4, select your Internet-connected network and scan the results. Pay attention to the following fields:

IP Address

Subnet Mask

Router (this is called "default gateway" in Windows, but the two terms are synonymous)

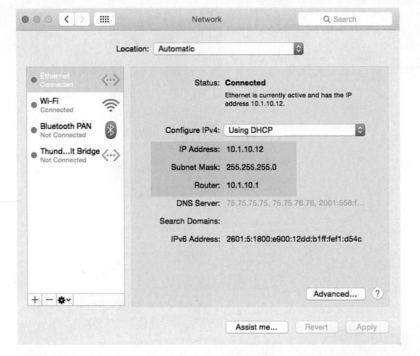

FIGURE 4.4 Viewing our network connection details in Apple OS X Mavericks.

NOTE

IPv4 Versus IPv6

Do you remember when I mentioned the scarcity of IP addresses? Specifically, I'm referring to IP version 4 (IPv4) addresses, which consist of four decimals between 0 and 255. IP version 6 (IPv6) is the next generation of the IP protocol, and has almost infinitely more public addresses available—the addresses themselves are 128 bits long as compared to 32 bits in IPv4, and the numbers are hexadecimal in IPv6 as opposed to decimal in IPv4.

We don't need to be concerned with IPv6 in this chapter, but since I'm sure you saw plenty of references to IPv6, I thought the subject was worth mentioning.

Viewing Our Router's Configuration

Now this is the tricky part because there exists a huge variety of router hardware. Are you a cable Internet subscriber, or do you use DSL? Or satellite? Does your Internet router have a built-in Wi-Fi access point, or have you "daisy-chained" a Wi-Fi router behind your Internet router? Sheesh—so potentially confusing.

Let's assume that our internal network devices connect to a single Comcast cable modem router. With very few exceptions, you're allowed to log in to your router directly to make configuration changes. You already know the router's private IP address; this is your computer's default gateway address.

Therefore, open a web browser and navigate to that address by using the web standard Hypertext Transfer Protocol (HTTP). For instance, here's what I need to type in my browser's address bar to reach my cable modem router:

```
http://10.1.10.1
```

My router's web-based console and logon screen is shown in Figure 4.5.

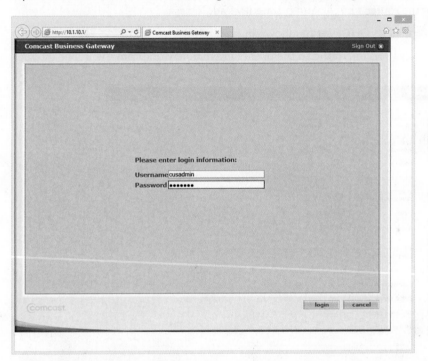

FIGURE 4.5   Most residential routers allow you to log in directly to make configuration changes.

TIP

If you neither know nor remember your router's login details, one thing you can do before filing a support ticket with your ISP is to check the Web. Sites such as RouterPasswords.com enable you to search on your router's manufacturer and discover the device's default administrative username and password. It's for this reason that you should change your router's password sooner rather than later! Any settings left at their default values are easy targets for malicious users.

After you're in the router's web interface, you can browse around to check settings and make changes. Here are some of the high points:

- Summary of the router's public and private IPv4 addresses
- Details concerning its DHCP setup (shown in Figure 4.6)
- Ability to forward specific traffic to the private internal network from the public Internet

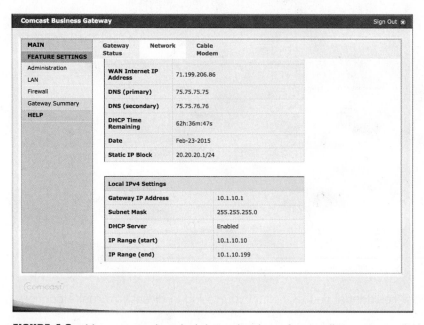

FIGURE 4.6 Your router's administrative interface tells you exactly how the device operates. Here we see the router's public and private IPv4 addresses.

Allowing Minecraft Traffic Through the Firewall

Your Internet-facing router acts as a firewall to protect your private internal network. A physical firewall is a divider that separates the passenger compartment from the engine compartment in an automobile; here the word "firewall" takes on a literal meaning.

In a TCP/IP computing context, a firewall is hardware and/or software that by default blocks all incoming Internet traffic to internal devices. The firewall is a good thing, believe me. The problem, if you want to call it that, is that your router's firewall will block any Internet-based player from accessing your internal Minecraft server. That is, unless you forward the appropriate port(s).

Ports

TCP/IP ports are cool because they allow your computer, which typically has a single IP address, to participate in all sorts of communication and not get "confused." This is even more important for your router, which is handling different traffic for different internal devices.

Think of it: You're browsing minecraftforum.net from your laptop, while your mom streams YouTube clips to her iPad, while your sister uploads files to her WordPress blog. That's a lot of network traffic, and it's all different.

Here's the deal: Different network services use different default port numbers. Here's a rundown of some of the most popular, well-known port numbers:

- HTTP (web browsing): 80
- HTTPS (secure HTTP): 443
- FTP (File Transfer Protocl): 21
- SMTP (e-mail): 25
- Minecraft (yeah, buddy!): 25565

Of the previously given ports, the only one I want you to memorize is 25565, because that is Minecraft's default port number.

What we want to do is forward inbound traffic on port 25565 to our Minecraft server that's located on the private internal network. Figure 4.7 summarizes port forwarding.

You might be wondering, "How can an Internet player get Minecraft traffic to me when my server has a private IP address? The router has NAT and a public IP address, but the router isn't the Minecraft server!"

We will give our Internet-based friends our router's public IP address, and they'll use that to connect to our Minecraft server. The router's NAT capability takes care of routing the port 25565 traffic to our server.

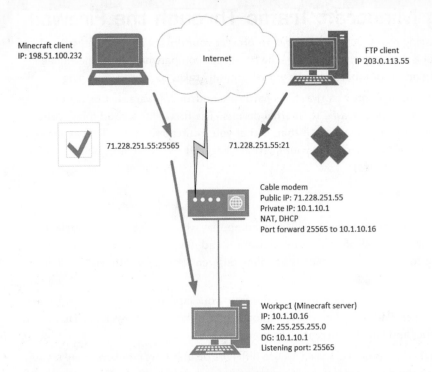

FIGURE 4.7 Schematic diagram showing how port forwarding works.

Let me walk you through Figure 4.7, because I packed a lot of information into that picture:

- Notice that the router has a port-forwarding rule defined such that it allows traffic on port 25565 and forwards it to IP 10.1.10.16, which is our Minecraft server.

- The Internet-based Minecraft client adds a server with the connection address 71.228.251.55:25565 (adding the colon and the port number shouldn't be necessary, but it's wise to use just to be safe) and is successful in connecting to the Workpc1 server.

- The FTP client, also Internet based, is unsuccessful in his or her attempt to establish a File Transfer Protocol (FTP) connection to an internal network resource because (a) the router blocks the traffic because it has no firewall exceptions defined; and (b) we don't have any FTP servers listening for connections in the first place.

I mentioned this in passing, but it bears repeating: You don't have to include the port number to the IP address if the service uses the default port. This is why you can type

```
http://yahoo.com
```

to reach yahoo.com, instead of this:

```
http://yahoo.com:80
```

Likewise, if your Minecraft server listens on its default port (whose value, you'll recall, is stored as the server-port property in your `server.properties` configuration file), then you shouldn't have to include the port. However, those who want to host more than one Minecraft server on the same box will indeed need to concern themselves with port numbers.

For instance, if I configured port forwarding for a second Minecraft server instance and I used port 25566, then I'd give this address to my Internet-based friends:

```
71.228.251.55:25566
```

Configuring Port Forwarding

Now let's configure our router for port forwarding!

TIP

Although the concept of port forwarding is identical no matter what router brand you have, each router manufacturer has a unique web-based management graphical user interface (GUI). Thus, I suggest that you hit up portforward.com to search for your router brand and receive detailed, step-by-step port-forwarding instructions. If you have a Linksys router, you can visit ui.linksys.com to play with fully functional router management console simulators.

FOLLOW ME!

Configuring Port Forwarding for Our Internal Minecraft Server

In this exercise we'll configure my Comcast cable modem to forward Minecraft traffic to my Workpc1 computer at IP address 10.1.10.16. You'll need to modify these steps slightly to conform to your particular router and IP addresses.

1 Log in to your router as an administrator and navigate to the page on which you can do port forwarding. In Figure 4.8, you can see the home page for my Comcast cable modem. I can click the handy-dandy Port Configuration button to jump directly to the port-forwarding page, or I can click Firewall and then Port Configuration to arrive at the same web page.

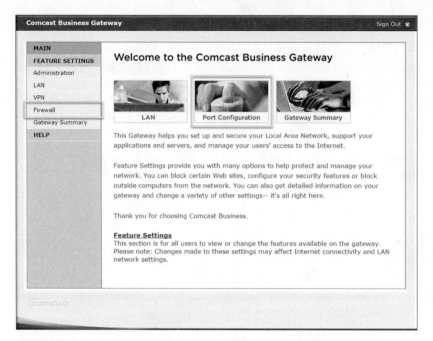

FIGURE 4.8 Router management interfaces sometimes place shortcuts to popular items such as port forwarding right on the home page.

2 On my router's Port Forwarding page, we click Add New to define a new port-forwarding rule.

3 On the Port Forwarding Add/Edit page, shown in Figure 4.9, I define my rule with the following properties:

Name: `Minecraft` (the name doesn't matter; this is just for your own reference).

Public: `25565-25565` (the range is to allow you to include more than one contiguous port number in one port-forwarding rule).

Private: `25565-25565`.

Protocol: `Both` (the two choices here are Transmission Control Protocol (TCP) and User Datagram Protocol (UDP); Mojang recommends that you forward both protocols).

IP Address: `10.1.10.16` (you'll substitute your Minecraft server's private IP address).

4 Click Apply to make the change go into effect.

5 On my router, you also have to check the Enable option to activate the port-forwarding rule.

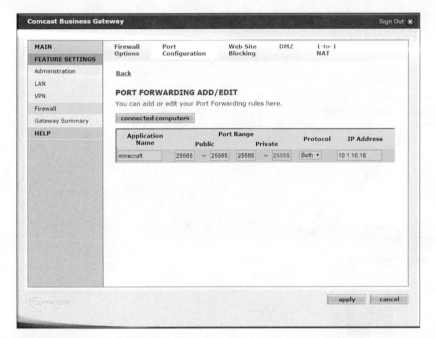

FIGURE 4.9   It's not as difficult as most Minecraft fans think to forward ports through your router or firewall.

Testing the Connection

Before we hand out our router's public IP address to our Minecraft buddies, we should check to verify that our router is actually forwarding port 25565 as expected.

CAUTION

Make sure that you start the Minecraft server on your internal network, or the port-forwarding test will fail. You actually need to have a service online and listening for connections for traffic to make it through your router/firewall.

TIP

The best way to test port forwarding is to use a computer from outside your home network. Many websites exist that can test port forwarding, but I recommend PortCheckTool.com, shown in Figure 4.10, because it both gives us our public IP address and tests port forwarding.

PortCheckTool.com - Port Check and IP detection Tool

Welcome to the Port Check Tool.

Let this tool help you check your ports! Want to know if your server is running? Now you can! Simply enter what port you want to verify into the empty box and click, "Check Your Port". A message will appear, notifying you if your port is blocked by a firewall or ISP.

Your Current Public IP Address is: 71.228.251.55

Success! I can see your service on 71.228.251.55 on port (25565)
Your ISP/Router/Firewall is **not** blocking port 25565.   X

Your IP?	71.228.251.55		Common Ports	
What Port?	25565		FTP	21
			SSH	22
	Check Your Port		Telnet	23
			SMTP	25
			Web	80

FIGURE 4.10 PortCheckTool.com serves a double duty of (a) giving you your router's public IP address; and (b) verifying that you configured port forwarding correctly.

To use PortCheckTool, simply plug in your router's public IP address in the Your IP field, enter 25565 in the What Port field, and click Check Your Port. As you can see in Figure 4.10, you'll get a "Success!" message if the website can get port 25565 traffic through your router.

If you get a failure, (a) make sure your Minecraft server is indeed running on your internal network; and (b) log in to your router and verify that the port-forwarding rule is present and enabled.

Let's Play!

Now run over to one of your Minecraft friends' homes, fire up the Minecraft client, and add your newly published Minecraft server as shown in Figure 4.11.

If all goes well, the newly added server will appear in the server list (see Figure 4.12), and you can join the server's world as usual. Awesomesauce!

Edit Server Info

Server Name

Zoey's MC Server

Server Address

71.228.251.55

Server Resource Packs: Prompt

Done

Cancel

FIGURE 4.11 You can try leaving the :25565 off the server address if you know that the target Minecraft server listens on the default port address.

Play Multiplayer

State's Server   0/5
State's Minecraft Server

a server   0/4
A Minecraft Server

Zoey's MC Server   0/20
Public Minecraft Server

Scanning for games on your local network
o 0 o

Join Server   Direct Connect   Add server

Edit   Delete   Refresh   Cancel

FIGURE 4.12 It feels pretty good to see your own Minecraft server in the Minecraft client's server list!

Using a Hostname Instead of an IP Address

Let's face it—dealing in "raw" IP addresses is tedious. Under the hood, your home router is itself a DHCP client of one of your ISP's DHCP servers. This means that your router's public IP address is likely to change at any time, which will immediately break your home-based Minecraft server.

I would much rather share the Minecraft server connection name

```
timwarner.ddns.net
```

than share this:

```
71.228.251.55:25566
```

Believe it or not, it is both easy and free to make this happen for your home-based Minecraft server. To do this, we need to create an account with a Dynamic Domain Name System (DDNS) service. These are the two companies I recommend:

- No-IP (http://noip.com)
- Dyn (http://dyn.com)

Understanding DNS and DDNS

DNS is a TCP/IP network service that translates user-friendly hostnames into IP addresses. For example, if you type

http://servers.minecraftforum.net

into your browser's address bar, the DNS server with which your computer is associated attempts to resolve the fully qualified domain name (FQDN), servers.minecraftforum.net, into the IP address of that particular web server.

The hostname part of the previous FQDN is "servers"; the domain name is "minecraftforum.net." The specifics of DNS name resolution are far outside the scope of this book; for our purposes, all you need to know is that companies like No-IP and Dyn will map an FQDN to your router's public IP address, and even adjust the mapping on the fly when your router's public IP changes.

Setting Up No-IP

We'll use No-IP in this example, but all the services work about the same.

FOLLOW ME!

Associate Your Minecraft Server By Hostname Instead of IP Address

In this exercise, we'll create a free No-IP account and then map our router's public IP address to an easy-to-remember hostname.

1 Point your web browser to https://www.noip.com/sign-up and register a new No-IP user account. Ignore or decline any "premium" offers; these DDNS companies make their money by adding features beyond what we need. If you're reading this while you're away from your computer, I show you the website in Figure 4.13.

2 Part of the signup involves choosing a domain name; as of this writing, ddns.net is the free option, so I'd suggest you choose that one. As a premium member, you get much more flexibility in your domain names.

You also can choose your own hostname; this is where I plugged in "timwarner." After all, if my Minecraft friends know me, they know my name and will always remember the name of my Minecraft server!

3 After you confirm your account via email and are all logged in, click Hosts/Redirects from the top navigation bar and then Manage Hosts from the side navigation.

4 Verify that your custom FQDN matches your router's public IP address. There's no magic going on here, by the way. No-IP discerned your public IP address by querying your current default gateway address. Therefore, you might need to manually modify the mapping if you created your account at school but need the mapping to hit your home router.

5 If you want, click Dynamic Update Client from the side navigation and download/install this software to your Minecraft server. What it does is check your router's public IP address every five minutes, and as soon as the client detects a change, it will update your No-IP mapping. Pretty cool, eh?

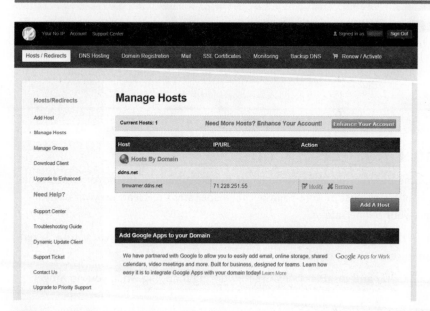

FIGURE 4.13 It's amazing that companies such as No-IP offer their dynamic DNS services free.

In Figure 4.14 you see that your players can now add your public Minecraft server to their client's server list by using a DNS name instead of a clunky IP address.

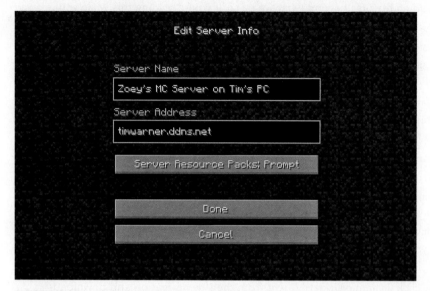

FIGURE 4.14 Your users will appreciate you for advertising your online Minecraft server with a hostname instead of an IP address.

> ## CAUTION
>
> Please understand that your players might still have to add the `:port` suffix to your hostname if you aren't running your Minecraft server by using the default port address.

Sweeping Up the Shavings

If you set up a home-based online Minecraft server for experimentation and/or educational purposes, then cool beans. Just be sure to take the proper steps to clean up your environment to maximize your online safety:

- Issue `/stop` in the Minecraft server console to halt the server and prevent it from listening for incoming connection requests.
- Log in to your router and disable your port-forwarding mapping when you no longer need it.
- Delete your No-IP mapping if you aren't using it anymore.

In IT, the security principle of "least service" says that if you don't need a service running on your network, turn it off and/or uninstall it. This way a malicious user can't abuse or exploit the service, because it simply isn't turned on in the first place.

The Bottom Line

I hope that you feel better about networking than you did before reading this chapter. To be sure, the knowledge and skills you have accrued by now will keep you in excellent stead as we proceed to the next phase of the book.

What is that phase, you ask? Well, it's time for us to say goodbye to the trusty Mojang "vanilla" Minecraft server and say hello to custom Minecraft servers in general, and the Bukkit platform in particular. See you then!

5

"If you don't like something, change it. If you can't change it, change your attitude."

—Maya Angelou, influential author and poet

Installing a Custom Minecraft Server

What You'll Learn in This Chapter:

- How to navigate the ultravolatile world of unofficial Minecraft servers
- How to set up a SpigotMC Minecraft multiplayer server
- How to install and configure the most popular Bukkit plugins
- How these plugins affect the Minecraft multiplayer game experience

The Minecraft vanilla server is nice because it's written by Mojang/Microsoft and has the company's official "blessing." On the other hand, the vanilla server in its present form cannot use server mods, which is what most server operators need in order to limit griefing, maximize their players' fun, and ease server administration.

In this chapter we'll begin to explore the wild, wooly world of third-party Minecraft server development. Because we're moving off the Mojang campus, as it were, we can't turn to them for support if something goes wrong with our server setup.

That said, I'll point you to the best Minecraft community spots on the Internet where your questions will be gratefully appreciated and answered by experts.

Let's get started!

Beginnings: It's a Wild, Wild West

A custom Minecraft server is a Java Archive (.jar) file that was written completely independently from the official Mojang Minecraft vanilla server.

These custom servers, of which there are many, are considered "unofficial" and are viewed neutrally (at best) to negatively (at worst) by the Mojang/Microsoft Minecraft team.

Bukkit is the application programming interface (API) that resulted in CraftBukkit, which was until late 2014 the world's de facto unofficial server. Minecraft server admins loved CraftBukkit because of its plugin architecture—you can completely customize the server in a way that's impossible with the vanilla server.

A lot of trouble occurred (to put it mildly) in the third quarter of 2014 that resulted in CraftBukkit's official disappearance from the Internet. Among the strange turns of events was the revelation that Mojang had actually purchased the Bukkit/CraftBukkit code base two years prior even though the rest of the world thought it was a public, community-supported project.

The Bukkit tale is a long, complicated story. All you need to know for our purposes is that CraftBukkit is dead and that other community development teams are making Minecraft servers that remain compatible with Bukkit plugins because those plugins are so valuable. Other groups, in particular the Sponge team (https://www.spongepowered.org/), are attempting to build a new unofficial Minecraft server from scratch that has no connection to Bukkit at all.

If you're truly interested in learning more about the Bukkit/Mojang fiasco, here are a few high-value links for your researching pleasure:

■ Bukkit: It's time to say... (http://bit.ly/1BuOHp8)

■ As the Mod Turns (http://bit.ly/1BuPeau)

■ Mojang and the Bukkit Project (http://bit.ly/1BuPruI)

If Not Bukkit, Then What?

The Bukkit ecosystem thrives to this day even though CraftBukkit was suddenly and unmercifully torched in late 2014. In point of fact, you can find all sorts of awesome Bukkit plugins all over the Net; most Minecraft server admins I know prefer to download Bukkit plugins from the Bukkit site (http://dev.bukkit.org/bukkit-plugins/).

Mojang has spoken (a bit cryptically) that it plans to give Minecraft an honest-to-goodness plugin architecture someday. However, Mojang did say emphatically that such an API will *not* be based on Bukkit.

The unofficial Minecraft server I chose to use in this book is SpigotMC (http://spigotmc. org). Here are my reasons:

■ The SpigotMC project is mature and has an active developer and player community.

■ The SpigotMC server itself is coded to improve server performance, which is always good news to your players.

■ The SpigotMC server is compatible with the Bukkit plugin ecosystem; thus, we can take advantage of the greatest plugins already in existence.

- The SpigotMC server is regularly updated to at least close to the current product Minecraft version.

Installing SpigotMC

The first step to build a SpigotMC server is to obtain the latest stable .jar file. Point your browser to spigotmc.org and click the Spigot Download link, as shown in Figure 5.1.

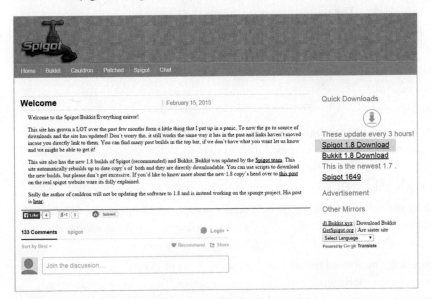

FIGURE 5.1 The SpigotMC development team does their best to match their server software with the latest Mojang release.

NOTE

The Minecraft modding community has been highly volatile since 2014. If you find that these instructions are no longer valid, then you may have to compile the Spigot server by hand. Instructions for making BuildTools can be found on the website at http://www.spigotmc.org/wiki/buildtools/. I'm sorry for any inconvenience, but it just goes with the territory.

Create a folder in your home folder (OS X) or the root of drive C: (Windows) called spigotserver, and pop your newly downloaded jar file in it. Next, rename your jar to something easy like spigot.jar.

As usual, you'll want to create your startup script. To refresh your memory, here is our Windows startup script, start.cmd:

```
@echo off
java -Xms1024M -Xmx1024M -XX:MaxPermSize=128M -jar spigot.jar
pause
```

The @echo off line prevents the Command Prompt window from showing the java command. The MaxPermSize property sets the PermGen space, which is memory reserved for long-term Minecraft objects. The pause statement keeps the Command Prompt window open instead of automatically closing it after the server starts.

Here is our OS X startup script, start.command:

```
#!/bin/bash
cd "$( dirname "$0" )"
java -Xms1024M -Xmx1024M -XX:MaxPermSize=128M -jar spigot.jar
```

The first line is what's called a "shebang" line, and points your Mac to the bash command interpreter. The second line sets your current location to the spigotserver folder.

Starting SpigotMC Server

Go ahead and start the server by double-clicking your startup script, accept the EULA, and then start again. The theme here is that setting up and starting SpigotMC is exactly the same procedure we use to set up and start the official Minecraft server.

As shown in Figure 5.2, you'll need to use the Command Prompt (Windows) or Terminal (OS X) session to perform management actions on your server. This is because SpigotMC doesn't use any Mojang proprietary code and therefore can't invoke the official Minecraft server's GUI.

> **NOTE**
>
> In the official Minecraft server console, you can issue commands with or without the slash (/) prefix. In the SpigotMC command-line console, you get an error if you include the slash.

To stop the SpigotMC server, simply type stop in the command window and press Enter or Return. You'll need have the server down to perform any maintenance.

```
                            C:\Windows\system32\cmd.exe                    _  □  ×
[09:14:51 INFO]: Preparing start region for level 2 (Seed: -7948577955968038375) ^
[09:14:52 INFO]: Preparing spawn area: 23%
[09:14:53 INFO]: Preparing spawn area: 46%
[09:14:54 INFO]: Preparing spawn area: 65%
[09:14:55 INFO]: Preparing spawn area: 89%
[09:14:55 INFO]: Done (30.827s)! For help, type "help" or "?"
>help
[09:16:15 INFO]: ----------                    --------------------------
[09:16:15 INFO]: Use /help [n] to get page n of help.
[09:16:15 INFO]: Aliases:
[09:16:15 INFO]: Bukkit:
[09:16:15 INFO]: Minecraft:
[09:16:15 INFO]: /achievement:
[09:16:15 INFO]: /ban:
[09:16:15 INFO]: /ban-ip:
[09:16:15 INFO]: /banlist:
[09:16:15 INFO]: /blockdata:
[09:16:15 INFO]: /clear:
[09:16:15 INFO]: /clone:
[09:16:15 INFO]: /debug:
[09:16:15 INFO]: /defaultgamemode:
[09:16:15 INFO]: /deop:
[09:16:15 INFO]: /difficulty:
[09:16:15 INFO]: /effect:
```

FIGURE 5.2 You'll need to be comfortable working from a Terminal/Command Prompt window because SpigotMC can't use the official Minecraft Server GUI.

Configuring SpigotMC

Take a look at Figure 5.3, which shows the contents of my `spigotserver` folder at right, and the partial contents of the `spigot.yml` configuration file at left. Lots of moving parts here, that's for sure.

FIGURE 5.3 Moving to the SpigotMC/Bukkit world means that you have more configuration files to work with (notice the `plugins` folder too—we'll have lots of fun with that later).

Let me help you to understand the three most important SpigotMC configuration files.

server.properties

There isn't much to say about `server.properties` because we've already learned what it is and how to use it. Feel free to customize the file as you see fit; the Minecraft Wiki (http://minecraft.gamepedia.com/Server.properties) has a full breakdown of each property and its allowed values.

> **TIP**
>
> Search the Web for advice on how to optimize Minecraft/Spigot configuration files. The general consensus is that you should set `allow-nether` to `false` if you don't need it, and set `view-distance` to 4 to improve game performance.

spigot.yml

The `spigot.yml` file is the primary SpigotMC configuration file. The easy-to-read file format is YAML, which humorously stands for "YAML Ain't Markup Language." See the `spigot.yml` page at the SpigotMC Wiki (http://www.spigotmc.org/wiki/spigot-configuration-spigot-yml/?redirect=spigot-configuration) for a full description of all its properties.

Let's set a simple option to give us a feel for how it works. First, find the following line in the `messages:` section:

```
unknown-command: Unknown command. Type "/help" for help.
```

Let's change this default message to something more friendly:

```
unknown-command: Say what? Type "/help" and learn.
```

bukkit.yml

Remember that SpigotMC is based on CraftBukkit, which in turn is based on the vanilla Minecraft server. One of SpigotMC's best-selling points is that the server can run all Bukkit plugins. Therefore, you use `bukkit.yml` to tweak Bukkit-related code. Read the BukkitWiki for more information on this file: http://wiki.bukkit.org/Bukkit.yml.

Testing the Player Experience

When you run the official Minecraft server and client, you never have to worry about Minecraft versions. That situation is much, much (did I say "much"?) different in the world of unofficial third-party Minecraft servers.

As a player, I'm sure you've been rejected from Minecraft server connections for one or both of the following reasons:

- Version mismatch between the Minecraft server and client
- Version mismatch between a Minecraft server and client mod

As a Minecraft custom server administrator, you need to constantly keep your eye on the ball in terms of knowing your Minecraft server version, your plugin versions, your Java version, and so forth.

To that point, I have a trivia question for you: What Minecraft version does your SpigotMC server run—can you find out at a glance?

One answer is to check for key lines of output when you start the SpigotMC console. Look here:

```
[13:01:03 INFO]: Starting minecraft server version 1.8
[13:01:04 INFO]: This server is running CraftBukkit
version git-Spigot-35348a5-ee6d0fa (MC: 1.8)
(Implementing API version 1.8-R0.1-SNAPSHOT)
```

We should be fine starting our Minecraft client with a version 1.8x profile. Before you do that, though, first make sure to OP yourself in the server console:

```
op TechTrainerTim
```

Next, let's log in to the multiplayer world and issue first a known command and then a bogus one to make sure that SpigotMC knows what it's doing:

```
/list
/lost
```

In Figure 5.4 you can see the results of the /list command in the chat pane, and then you can see our custom message. It looks like SpigotMC is behaving just fine thus far!

And now for the moment that many of you have been waiting for: Bukkit plugins!

There are 1/3 players online:
TechTrainerTim
Say what? Type "/help" and learn.

FIGURE 5.4 SpigotMC gives the OP so much more control over how Minecraft is experienced by your players.

Introducing Bukkit Plugins

Speaking generically, a plugin is software that doesn't stand alone, but is installed as a part of a larger software product. Specifically, Bukkit plugins are Java `.jar` files that were written to extend the functionality of the CraftBukkit server.

A plugin is different from a mod, which we'll cover in the next chapter, because plugins can't add any new assets to Minecraft. By contrast, Minecraft mods can fundamentally change the overall look and feel of the game.

Describing the Most Popular Plugins

Do you use Google Chrome? Chrome is my favorite web browser for many reasons, but its extensibility is something I dearly love. JavaScript developers create extensions (which can be considered plugins, I suppose), and you can view the top-rated and most popular ones at the Google Chrome Extension Gallery (https://chrome.google.com/webstore/category/extensions).

Bukkit plugins are hosted all over the world, so you'll need to cast your net wider than one website to get ideas. Here are a few popular Bukkit plugin repositories to get you started:

- Curse's Top Minecraft Bukkit Plugins: http://www.curse.com/bukkit-plugins/minecraft/downloads

- Bukkit's Plugin Index: http://dev.bukkit.org/bukkit-plugins/

- BukGet: https://bukget.org

The Bukkit.org Plugins index in shown in Figure 5.5.

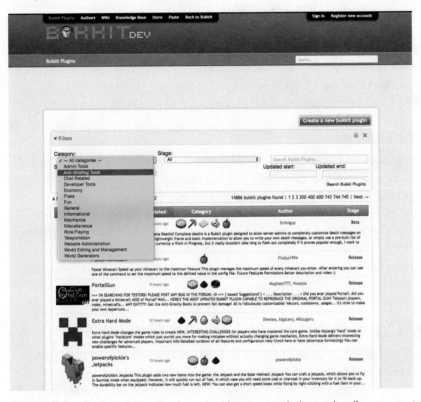

FIGURE 5.5 Any Bukkit plugin repository worth its salt allows you to filter the list to suit your preferences.

In my experience and research, I found the following Bukkit plugins to be essential to the conscientious Minecraft server administrator:

ClearLagg (http://dev.bukkit.org/bukkit-plugins/clearlagg/): Removes unnecessary elements from your shared world to reduce latency and improve performance.

Essentials (http://dev.bukkit.org/bukkit-plugins/essentials/): Mashup of various administration helps, including chat/nickname control, moderation, economy, and so forth.

WorldGuard (http://dev.bukkit.org/bukkit-plugins/worldguard/): Protects your world against griefing; enable or disable Minecraft features.

PermissionsEx (http://dev.bukkit.org/bukkit-plugins/permissionsex/): Called PEX for short; gives you granular control over game permissions for users, moderators, and OPs.

WorldEdit (http://dev.bukkit.org/bukkit-plugins/worldedit/): Gives you much greater control of your world from a manipulation standpoint (many of the biggest Minecraft builds in the [real] world were made with WorldEdit).

Multiverse-Core (http://www.curse.com/bukkit-plugins/minecraft/multiverse-core): Enables you to host multiple worlds in the context of a single SpigotMC server instance.

I hesitate to give you specific SpigotMC version dependencies in the previous list because the development community is so volatile. Your keys to success in the Bukkit plugin arena are (a) finding a plugin repository that stays current with new versions; and (b) reading the full plugin documentation before you attempt an installation. We'll get into that stuff in a moment.

A Question of Balance

Here's some good, real-world advice from me to you: Please be careful which plugins you choose to install on your server, and avoid installing too many plugins. How many is too many? You can quickly answer this question by periodically examining your SpigotMC plugins folder and asking yourself, "Does this plugin actually help me as an admin and help my players have a better play experience?" If the answer is no, remove the plugin from the directory and restart the server.

You need to find a balance between improving your server and "weighing it down" too much, resource-wise, by installing too many and/or the wrong plugins. Just some food for thought.

Installing, Configuring, and Using Bukkit Plugins

In this chapter we'll install Essentials as our case study plugin (actually a suite of plugins) because most Minecraft server admins find Essentials, well, essential to hosting a Minecraft server. Moreover, Essentials runs just fine in Minecraft v1.8, and is a stable/mature product in any event.

Obtaining Essentials: RTFM

In this "wild west" of Bukkit plugin development, it can be a challenge sometimes figuring out which site is best for downloading a plugin.

For instance, here are the four most reputable repositories I've used for obtaining the Essentials plugin:

- Essentials Project Page: http://wiki.mc-ess.net/wiki/Main_Page
- SpigotMC: http://www.spigotmc.org/resources/essentials.24/
- Curse: http://www.curse.com/bukkit-plugins/minecraft/essentials
- Dev.bukkit.org: http://dev.bukkit.org/bukkit-plugins/essentials/

The term "RTFM" is something we techie geeks define as "Read the Friendly Manual" (although the third word is often substituted for another non-family-friendly one).

Therefore, be sure to read as much documentation on a plugin as you can before you commit to downloading and installing it.

As I've stated earlier, Essentials is actually a collection of five separate, but interrelated, .jar files:

- **Essentials.jar**: More than 100 general-purpose commands for OPs and players.

- **EssentialsAntiBuild.jar**: Control which players can break, use, or place blocks.

- **EssentialsChat.jar**: Reformat chat pane and contents.

- **EssentialsProtect.jar**: Enable or disable world elements.

- **EssentialsSpawn.jar**: Control where players spawn in the world.

Let's go to the Bukkit.org page (http://dev.bukkit.org/bukkit-plugins/essentials/) to download Essentials. If you read the "fine print" in the Facts pane, you'll be surprised (although you shouldn't be) to notice that Essentials might not be compatible with Minecraft v1.8. In Figure 5.6, you can see that we need SpigotMC v1.7.2. Shucks!

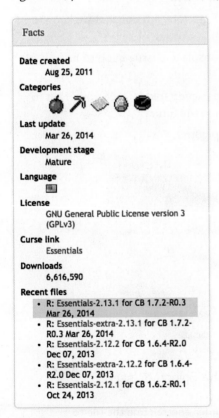

FIGURE 5.6   You need to resign yourself to running an older version of SpigotMC if you want the best plugins.

CAUTION

You know the old saying: You can find anything you want on the Internet. To that point, I'm sure if you do enough digging you'll find someone who shoehorned Essentials (or any other plugin) to work with the current Minecraft/Spigot versions. Be careful of downloading from nonreputable sources because you put your online safety and the stability of your Minecraft server at risk.

Back to the drawing board, right? Not really. It's pretty darned easy to pivot your SpigotMC server. Here's how to roll it back to v1.7.2.

FOLLOW ME!

Changing Your SpigotMC Server Version On the Fly

In this brief exercise we'll replace our current SpigotMC version with one that we know is compatible with the Essentials plugin pack.

1 If your SpigotMC server is still running, go to the console and issue `stop` to bring it down.

2 Move the existing `spigot.jar` out of your `spigotserver` folder; it's a good idea to keep it around just in case you want to use it again in the future.

3 Download the latest v1.7x release of Spigot from spigotmc.org; I point out the correct link on their home page in Figure 5.7.

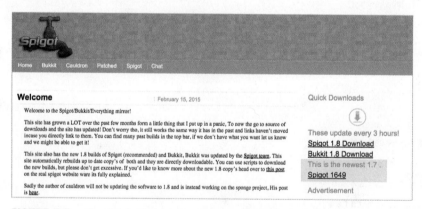

FIGURE 5.7   Downloading a previous version of the SpigotMC server.

4 Move the v1.7 Spigot jar to your `spigotserver` folder and rename the file to `spigot.jar`. This way we don't have to reconfigure our startup script.

5 Start up the server as usual. Because SpigotMC detects a change in its environment, you'll be prompted to confirm server startup in the console window; I show you what this looks like in Figure 5.8.

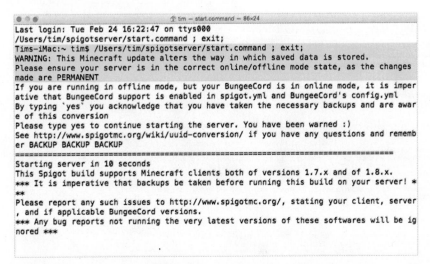

```
●●●                             ⬆ tim — start.command — 86×24
Last login: Tue Feb 24 16:22:47 on ttys000
/Users/tim/spigotserver/start.command ; exit;
Tims-iMac:~ tim$ /Users/tim/spigotserver/start.command ; exit;
WARNING: This Minecraft update alters the way in which saved data is stored.
Please ensure your server is in the correct online/offline mode state, as the changes
made are PERMANENT
If you are running in offline mode, but your BungeeCord is in online mode, it is imper
ative that BungeeCord support is enabled in spigot.yml and BungeeCord's config.yml
By typing `yes` you acknowledge that you have taken the necessary backups and are awar
e of this conversion
Please type yes to continue starting the server. You have been warned :)
See http://www.spigotmc.org/wiki/uuid-conversion/ if you have any questions and rememb
er BACKUP BACKUP BACKUP
==================================================================================
Starting server in 10 seconds
This Spigot build supports Minecraft clients both of versions 1.7.x and of 1.8.x.
*** It is imperative that backups be taken before running this build on your server! *
**
Please report any such issues to http://www.spigotmc.org/, stating your client, server
, and if applicable BungeeCord versions.
*** Any bug reports not running the very latest versions of these softwares will be ig
nored ***
```

FIGURE 5.8 Downloading a previous version of the SpigotMC server.

6 When you start your Minecraft client, be sure to edit your profile to play Minecraft v1.7.2 (or possibly a later version of v1.7, with v1.7.10 being the final release before v1.8).

Now you're safe to download the Essentials plugin pack. The file usually arrives to your computer as a `.zip` archive. Double-click the `.zip` and extract its contents to your `spigotserver/plugins` folder as shown in Figure 5.9.

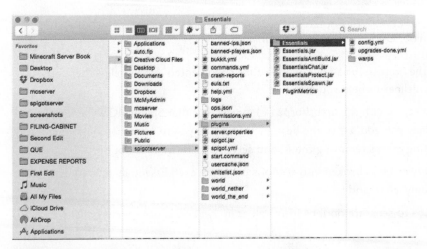

FIGURE 5.9 The Essentials plugin pack is installed and ready to rumble.

Configuring Essentials

Fortunately, we don't have to horse around with separate .yml configuration files for each Essentials pack component. Instead, we have a single file named config.yml that's located in your spigotserver/plugins/Essentials folder as shown in Figure 5.10.

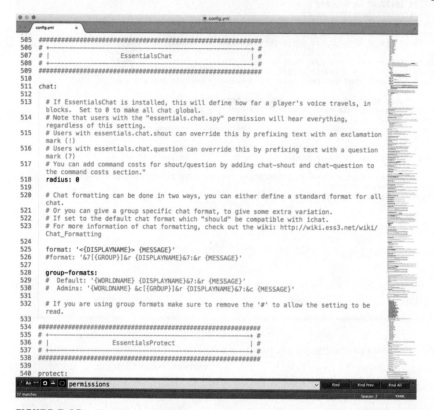

FIGURE 5.10 The Essentials config.yml has the same format as the Spigot configuration files, and is very well documented.

You'll find that the config.yml file is wonderfully documented. Nonetheless, here are some general guidelines to help you out:

- Any line that starts with the octothorpe (#) means that that SpigotMC will ignore that line. When you add a # to the beginning of a line, you're "commenting it out." Uncommenting means removing the #, and serves to activate that option.

- The config.yml file is broken into sections based on each Essentials functionality element (economy, chat, and so on).

- Never use tabs to separate options from values in .yml files; use spaces only.

- Big files like this can sometimes make it difficult to find the option you're looking for. You can start most text editors' search components with a Ctrl+F (Cmd+F on OS X). Next, type part of the option you're looking for, press Enter/Return, and you're all set.

- If you're using Sublime Text, you can navigate through the file easily by dragging and dropping the box that appears on the right window border.

It takes a lot of patience, practice, and experimentation to find the config.yml settings that work well for your Minecraft server. Let me share with you a number of Essentials options that I like, along with suggested values and a justification:

ops-name-color: This formats OP name color differently from the rest of the player population. Get the color code values from http://ess.khhq.net/mc/; I set mine to e (yellow) to make my OP name "pop" in the chat pane.

teleport-cooldown: This prevents users from bogging down your server by issuing multiple /home or /tp commands. I set mine to 60 to force users to wait 60 seconds before using these commands again.

item-spawn-blacklist: Prevents the /give of potentially troublesome items. Get Minecraft IDs from http://minecraft-ids.grahamedgecombe.com/; I set mine to 46,11,10, which prevents the /give of TNT, still lava, and flowing lava.

kits: This is a really cool feature. You can build collections of items (basic tools along with a bit of food, for instance), and make them available to your players. More information on kits here: http://wiki.ess3.net/wiki/Kits.

signs: Again, an awesome feature. These look like ordinary Minecraft signs, but contain code that triggers when a player interacts with the sign. Remove the # from any signs that you want available in your shared world; I uncommented them all.

auto-afk; auto-afk-kick: AFK stands for "away from keyboard." The first option changes player status after a specified interval (in seconds) elapses; the second option boots the player after an additional time-out period.

custom-join-message: Welcome your players with a personal message. I set mine to "Hello and welcome to my SpigotMC server!"

custom-quit-message: I set mine to "So long, and thanks for all the fish!" (That's a Douglas Adams reference, by the way.)

starting-balance; command-costs; currency-symbol: The Essentials economy system makes for a fascinating Minecraft multiplayer world. I set the starting-balance to 100, which means that joining players begin their journey with that amount of credit. The command-costs section allows you to put prices on various actions. This is a complex topic that could be a small book in itself; read the Essentials Wiki (http://wiki.ess3.net/wiki/Essentials_Economy) for more information.

prevent:spawn: I set ender_dragon to true here so that my players won't be able to spawn ender dragons.

blacklist: We can specify Minecraft block IDs (reference: http://minecraft-ids. grahamedgecombe.com/) that players aren't allowed to place. The entry placement `10,11,46,327` disallows the placement of flowing lava, still lava, TNT, and lava bucket blocks, respectively.

kit:tools: Here we can give players a kit automatically when they log in to our server. I commented this line out because I want to use signs or the `/kit` command to issue kits to players.

Testing the Gameplay Experience

Time to test! After starting the SpigotMC server, we'll OP TechTrainerTim by typing the following in the Terminal console:

```
>op TechTrainerTim
[11:38:30 INFO]: CONSOLE: Opped TechTrainerTim
```

Next, we'll fire up our two Minecraft clients, making sure to start with v1.7.2. You can verify the Minecraft version on the home page as shown in Figure 5.11.

FIGURE 5.11 Running older versions of Minecraft is a way of life when you're using most unofficial servers.

As Dorothy said, "Toto, we're not in Kansas anymore!" Likewise, you can tell you're dealing with a very different kind of Minecraft server upon first login. Examine Figure 5.12 to see what I'm talking about.

FIGURE 5.12 The combination of SpigotMC and Essentials makes for a totally customizable Minecraft multiplayer gaming environment.

In Figure 5.13 you can see that our OP account shows up in yellow, just as we specified in config.yml.

FIGURE 5.13 Essentials makes it easier for players to identify OPs.

Next, let's play with signs and the Essentials economy system. First, let's give TechTrainer-Tim a stack of signs:

```
/give TechTrainerTim sign
```

We'll place a sign nearby (I trust you've done that before), and use Essentials syntax to denote the sign type, its permissions, and the cost per use. Look at Figure 5.14.

FIGURE 5.14 Essentials makes it easier for players to identify OPs.

The first line denotes the sign type (check the `config.yml` to refresh your memory regarding sign type options). The second line specifies what the sign gives or does. Here I'm specifying the diamond tools kit that already exists in `config.yml`. The third line says that anyone on my server can access sign contents. The fourth line says that we charge the player 50 units per sign use.

From my zoey2010 session we'll check our currency balance:

```
/balance
Balance: $100
```

Cool! Now we'll walk to the sign, right-click, and see what happens, as shown in Figure 5.15.

FIGURE 5.15 Remember that $50 is a small price to pay for a suite of stone tools (at least for beginners!).

The built-in economy tools, even before your customization, are awesome. For instance, let's say Zoey gets desperate for funds and decides to sell her stone sword:

```
/sell stone_sword 1
$2.50 has been added to your account.
Sold for $2.50 (1 stone_sword at $2.50 each)
```

As an OP, you can do stuff like reward players for killing mobs, or set up swap meets. If I haven't told you this already, I love Minecraft!

Make sure to run /help and page through the results to see all the new commands. For instance, we can easily publish our server rules:

```
/rules
Error: File rules.txt does not exist. Creating one for you.
```

The rules.txt file is created in plugins/Essentials; customize it as you see fit! The default rules are shown in Figure 5.16.

FIGURE 5.16   Your players need to know your rules before they can be expected to behave appropriately. As you get more comfortable with SpigotMC and Essentials, you'll want to know more about what's available, command-wise. Check out the Essentials Wiki (http://ess.khhq.net/wiki/Command_Reference) and play with the different commands!

The Bottom Line

Are you grateful or angry that in this chapter I turned your understanding of Minecraft server on its head and provided you with an entirely new way to manage your multiplayer server? I'm hoping for the former, of course.

For your homework assignment, I'd like you to install another popular SpigotMC plugin and learn how it works. I'd suggest PermissionsEx so that you can take steps to better customize what actions are and are not allowed in your shared world, as well as who can perform such actions.

In the next chapter we'll continue our trek through the unofficial Minecraft server weeds by bringing server mods to the table. My five-year-old daughter, Zoey, absolutely loves both Pokémon and Minecraft. By installing the Pixelmon mod (http://pixelmonmod.com/), she can have the best of both worlds! More to come—see you in the next few pages.

6

"The only thing that will redeem mankind is cooperation."

—Bertrand Russell, British philosopher and social critic

Integrating Mods into Your Minecraft Server

What You'll Learn in This Chapter:

- Introducing Cauldron
- Installing a mod
- Experimenting with modpacks and launchers
- Finding quality client-side mods

It's difficult enough to describe how the original Minecraft works when I'm talking about the game with family, friends, or colleagues. After all, the game morphs to the player's style and preferences. If you want to focus on builds, you can do that. The same can be said for farming, animal breeding, dungeon exploring, or redstone circuitry.

If you can believe it, mods put another "coat of paint" on Minecraft. For example, you can install mods that transform your Minecraft multiplayer world into a Dungeons and Dragons–type role-playing game (RPG), a Pokémon adventure, a dystopian science-fiction fantasy, and so forth. Mods are awesome.

In this chapter we'll learn how to use Cauldron, another unofficial server whose primary claim to fame is that it runs both Minecraft Forge mods and Bukkit plugins. Enough with the preliminaries—we have a lot of work to do.

Introducing Cauldron

I have good news and bad news. The bad news first: Although the Cauldron project page remains online (http://cauldron.minecraftforge.net/), the download links have been removed as of this writing in spring 2015. It seems that Cauldron was swept into the Mojang-community firestorm along with both SpigotMC and CraftBukkit.

The good news is that the Cauldron project has been forked and is still available over the Net by committed developers who believe in the platform. By the way, when an open-source project is copied and managed by a separate group of people, that project is said to have been forked. This tree-branch structure is one of the magical aspects of open-source software.

Cauldron is a sort of "hybrid" Minecraft server that allows admins to use both Bukkit plugins (such as SpigotMC) and Forge mods (such as Minecraft Forge).

Minecraft Forge in a Nutshell

Minecraft Forge is a client/server API for Minecraft modding. A mod, short for "modification," is code that actually can modify (change) core Minecraft assets. Compare a mod with a plugin, which is smaller software that's "bolted onto" Minecraft server and simply adds functionality to what's already there.

In case I never defined API: An application programming interface can be viewed as a set of connectivity rules that programmers follow in order to connect two different services. With regard to Minecraft Forge, the API stands between the Minecraft server and one or more Forge mods.

The "client/server" piece of the definition refers to the fact that we need to install Forge both on our Minecraft server and in the Minecraft client. I need to emphasize that: *Every user who wants to play on your Forge server first needs to download and install the Forge client.* This extra requirement might reduce the number of server players you receive from the Internet. On the other hand, the awesome gameplay experiences you can offer by combining Bukkit and Forge might make your server more desirable than it would be otherwise.

As you can see in Figure 6.1, players who try to log in to your Cauldron server without the Forge client installed get hung up indefinitely on the "Logging in" screen.

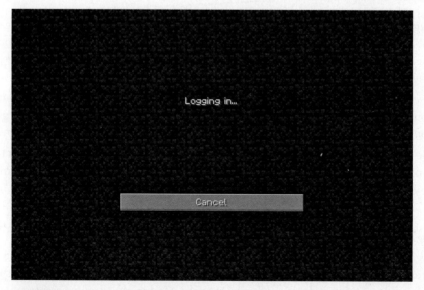

FIGURE 6.1   The vanilla Minecraft server environment we'll use for all examples in this chapter.

Installing the Forge Client

If you haven't already done so, please visit http://files.minecraftforge.net/ and download Minecraft Forge for your target Minecraft version. As of this writing, v1.7.10 is the best version to try. This is shown in Figure 6.2.

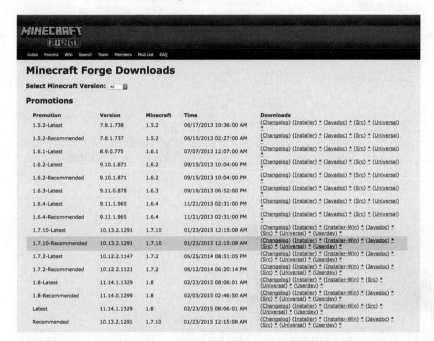

FIGURE 6.2   Minecraft Forge offers you client/server downloads for Windows and OS X. Note that you can choose your target Minecraft game version.

Note that Minecraft Forge uses a "universal" installation model in which the same installer can install either the server or the client version. The Installer link on their web page downloads the OS X–friendly `.jar` file; the Installer-Win link gives you a traditional `.exe` file. The first screens from the universal installer are shown in Figure 6.3.

When you start your Minecraft client, open the Profile menu and choose the Forge profile that the installer helpfully gave you. You can confirm Forge client installation on the Minecraft home page. I did a "mashup" screenshot in Figure 6.4 so that you can see what's going on.

FIGURE 6.3 You use the same program to install the client and server Minecraft Forge versions. However, Cauldron includes the Forge server bits so we don't need to do it here.

FIGURE 6.4 Minecraft Forge helpfully creates a game profile for you that is matched to a particular game version.

Because we don't yet have any Forge mods actually installed on our server, simply having the client ready is a good start, but nothing more.

Let's turn our attention to installing our first Cauldron server.

Getting Cauldron Up and Running

Now that we've had experience with installing both the vanilla Minecraft server and SpigotMC, you should have no trouble installing Cauldron. Actually, the hardest piece of the process is probably finding a decent `.jar` file download link!

FOLLOW ME!

Install the Cauldron Server

In this exercise we'll set up the Cauldron Minecraft server, which allows us to install both Forge mods as well as Bukkit plugins.

1 Point your web browser to http://sourceforge.net/projects/cauldron-unofficial/ files/?source=navbar and browse into your target version. In this book I chose the `1.7.10-latest` folder.

2 Inside the version folder download both the server `.jar` and the libraries `.zip` file. For my part, I downloaded these:

`cauldron-1.7.10-1.1236.05.212-server.jar`

`libraries-1.1236.05.zip`

3 Create a folder named `cauldron` (or any other name of your choosing) in an easy-to-find spot on your computer's hard drive.

4 Move the `.jar` file into the `cauldron` folder, and unzip the libraries archive into it as well. Among other things, the libraries ZIP file includes a copy of the vanilla Minecraft server jar. As it happens, Cauldron requires that the vanilla server be present within the Cauldron installation folder.

5 Create a startup script. I simply copied and pasted my SpigotMC startup script. Don't forget to rename the `.jar` file to match your Cauldron `.jar`.

6 Run the startup script, accept the `EULA.txt`, and restart the server. Your cauldron folder will fill up with assets. Take note of the plugins and mods folders—we'll make heavy use of them soon!

The Forge-enabled end-user experience at this point is pretty plain vanilla (pun intended). Let's first do a "proof of concept" to show that Cauldron can in fact run Bukkit plugins, and then we'll turn our full attention to Minecraft mods.

First, Our Plugin Proof of Concept

Do you remember the PermissionsEx (PEX) plugin from the preceding chapter? I thought we'd install and configure PEX on our Cauldron server as a proof of concept to demonstrate that Cauldron can in fact run Bukkit plugins.

If you haven't already downloaded PEX, do so from the Bukkit website: http://dev.bukkit. org/bukkit-plugins/permissionsex/. Make sure that you choose the .jar that corresponds with Minecraft 1.7.10.

CAUTION

Please be careful when you download any Minecraft community resources. Sadly, some users and groups host their files on AdFly and other sites that are prone to pop-up advertisements (at best) and drive-by downloads (at worst). To be as safe as possible, use a quality browser such as Google Chrome and install ad-blocking extensions.

Downloaded the .jar in your cauldron/plugins folder just as we did with SpigotMC.

PermissionsEx Quick Start

Recall that PermissionsEx is part of the Essentials plugin pack. Specifically, PermissionsEx allows Minecraft server operators to implement role-based access control (RBAC) in their worlds.

For example, we might want to define a group named Players for our regular players, and define which actions the players can and cannot perform in our shared world.

Moreover, we might want to delegate game administration to other players, but not give those moderators/junior OPs full server privileges. You can do that kind of thing with PEX.

After placing the PermissionsEx .jar in the plugins folder, start Cauldron, and then /stop it. You'll find a new PermissionsEx folder inside cauldron/plugins that contains permissions.yml, which is as you'd suspect the PEX configuration file to be.

Thanks to the YouTuber and skilled instructor GhostGrowlithe (https://www.youtube.com/watch?v=uWANbaMXj0M), I have a fully populated sample permissions.yml file. Nab the file from Ghost's YouTube page and overwrite your local copy.

Take a look at Figure 6.5 and I'll briefly explain how it's set up.

```yaml
permissions.yml                              × 

1   groups:
2     Player:
3       default: true
4       permissions:
5       - essentials.signs.use.*
6       - essentials.warp.*
7       - essentials.tpahere
8       - essentials.delhome
9       - essentials.home
10      - essentials.sethome.multiple.default
11      - essentials.warp.list
12      - essentials.warp
13      - essentials.spawn
14      - essentials.realname
15      - essentials.rules
16      - essentials.msg
17      - essentials.help.*
18      - essentials.baltop
19      - essentials.balancetop
20      - essentials.balance
21      - essentials.bal
22      - essentials.money
23      - essentials.helpop
24      - essentials.tpdeny
25      - essentials.list
26      - essentials.tpaccept
27      - essentials.tpa
28      - modifyworld.*
29      prefix: '&a[Player] &f'
30    Trusted:
31      prefix: '&6[Trusted] &f'
32      inheritance:
33      - Player
34    Builder:
35      prefix: '&2[Builder] &f'
36      inheritance:
37      - Player
38    Helper:
39      prefix: '&e[Helper] &f'
40      inheritance:
41      - Player
42    Moderator:
43      prefix: '&b[Mod] &f'
44      permissions:
45      - essentials.mute
46      - essentials.ban
47      - essentials.kick
48      - essentials.kick.notify
49      - essentials.ban.notify
50      - essentials.tempban
51      inheritance:
52      - Player
53    Admin:
54      prefix: '&c[Admin] &f'
55      permissions:
56      - '*'
57    Owner:
58      prefix: '&9[Owner] &f'
59      permissions:
60      - '*'
61
```

Line 1, Column 1   Spaces: 4   YAML

FIGURE 6.5 Using simple syntax, we can define true role-based access control for our Minecraft server by using the PEX plugin.

- We have seven groups defined, from Player (the default group) to Owner (who has all permissions).

- Be careful with the indentations; YAML files use indents to differentiate different data.

- Note that we specify Minecraft permissions by using an `essentials.*` syntax; for more details please read the PEX documentation at https://github.com/PEXPlugins/PermissionsEx/wiki.

Testing the Plugin

Save your `permissions.yml` changes and start Cauldron again. You can do all your PEX administration from within the server console. For this test, don't OP yourself. Instead, let's play with the default PEX roles.

FOLLOW ME!

Experimenting with PermissionsEx

Yes, I know that this chapter is supposed to be about mods—we'll get there, trust me. In the meantime, let's play with PermissionsEx; I'm positive that you'll find the exercise worth your effort.

1 In your Cauldron command-line console, let's verify that the plugin is installed by typing `pl` (/pl in-game):

```
pl
[19:16:32 INFO]: Plugins (5): PermissionsEx, Essentials,
 EssentialsProtect, EssentialsSpawn, EssentialsChat
```

Yep, it looks like we're good to go.

2 Now let's get a run of all the PermissionsEx commands:

```
pex
```

I omitted the output from that one because, as I'm sure you noticed, PEX has a lot of commands.

3 You might be logged on with OP privileges already, which overrides PEX permissions. In the console you can de-OP yourself:

```
deop techtrainertim
[19:57:52 INFO]: CONSOLE: De-opped techtrainertim
```

4 Fire up your Minecraft client and start a v1.7.10 session with the Forge profile. Join your multiplayer server and verify that the custom `permissions.yml` file we added earlier works. You should see something similar to what is shown in Figure 6.6.

In particular, look at the [Player] prefix on our username. The other chat elements you see are proof that at least on my server, I'm running other Essentials plugins (you can add 'em too if you like Essentials—I love that plugin pack so much).

We can verify our world's default group this way from the console:

```
pex default group world
[20:29:53 INFO]: Default groups in world "world" are:
[20:29:53 INFO]:   - Player
```

5 Remember that the Player group doesn't have much ability in our world. For instance, let's try to change the time of day:

```
/time set day
You do not have access to that command.
```

6 From the console, let's promote my TechTrainerTim account to be a member of the Admin group:

```
pex group Admin user add TechTrainerTim
[20:31:31 INFO]: User TechTrainerTim added to Admin !
```

7 You can immediately see the results in-game. For instance, my player now shows up this way in the chat window:

```
[Admin] TechTrainerTim
```

8 Now I can issue server commands all day long:

```
/time set day
[20:32:08 INFO]: TechTrainerTim issued server command: /time set day
```

FIGURE 6.6 By using PEX, we make it easier for our players to know who to ask if they have questions or concerns because the user role appears directly onscreen.

Now for the Good Stuff—Installing a Mod

The toughest thing about this part of the chapter is choosing a mod for us to use as a case study! The reason for this is simple: There exist so many cool mods, some of which seem to be as big as the original Minecraft game.

Here's a quick survey of some of my favorite modpacks:

Railcraft (http://www.railcraft.info/): A complete reimagining of the Minecraft minecart system.

BuildCraft (http://www.mod-buildcraft.com/): Build complex machines for automation and beyond.

IndustrialCraft2 (http://www.industrial-craft.net/): Another building/machining mod.

Tinkers Construct (http://www.curse.com/mc-mods/minecraft/tinkers-construct): Takes the original Minecraft's crafting interface to another level entirely.

Pixelmon (http://pixelmonmod.com/): Pokémon + Minecraft.

TIP

If you like the engineering-oriented mods I suggest here, you might want to investigate Tekkit (http://www.technicpack.net/modpack/tekkitmain.552547), which combines a number of these mods into a single, unified modpack and launcher.

NOTE

My fellow Que author Stephen O'Brien teaches you how to use most of the mods I mention here in his wonderful book, *The Advanced Strategy Guide to Minecraft*. Please check it out and accelerate your learning!

Installing RailCraft

For our purposes let's try Railcraft as a test case. Head on over to the project home page (http://www.railcraft.info/releases/) and download the release that corresponds to your target Minecraft version. I found that Railcraft supports Minecraft v1.7.10 just fine.

On your Cauldron server, put the Railcraft `.jar` in the `cauldron/mods` folder.

Next, and this is important, put the same `.jar` file in the `mods` folder of each Minecraft client. If you don't do this, the player will see the error shown in Figure 6.7.

FIGURE 6.7 Always remember that your players need to have versions and components that match what's installed on your server; that pertains to Minecraft, Bukkit plugins, and mods.

The `mods` location for Minecraft client depends on your operating system:

Windows: `%appdata%\.minecraft\mods`

OS X: `/Users/<username>/Application Support/minecraft/mods`

In Windows, `%appdata%` is an environment variable that jets you to the following location on your hard drive:

`C:\Users\<username>\AppData\Roaming`

Now shut down and restart your Cauldron server to make sure that it initializes Railcraft.

Restart your Minecraft client. From the home page, click Mods. Recall that the mere presence of this new button (shown in Figure 6.8) lets us know that we're, well, modding the way in which vanilla Minecraft functions.

As shown in Figure 6.9, you can verify your installed Railcraft version and its availability status. Of course, you can also check runtime status in your Cauldron command-line console.

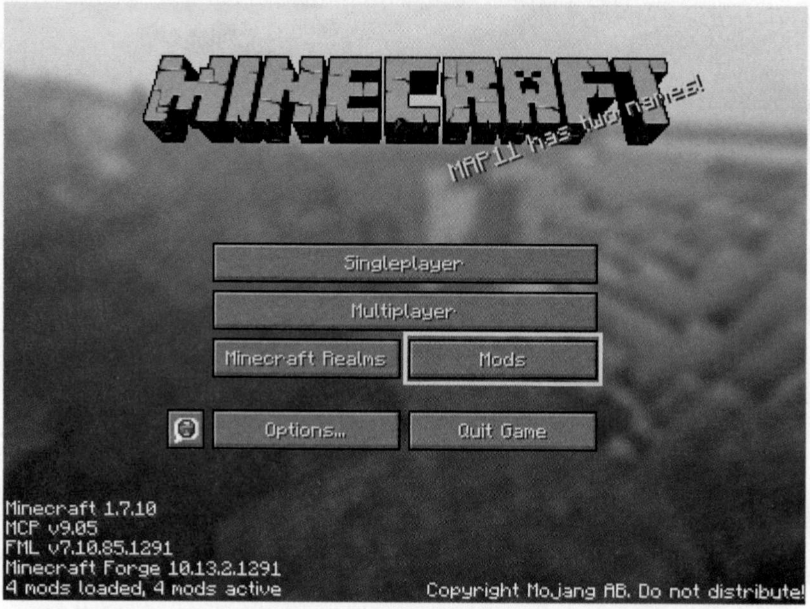

FIGURE 6.8 Notice the Mods button, which lets us know that our Minecraft client exists far off the Mojang reservation.

FIGURE 6.9 Railcraft is installed on the client and available for use.

Testing the Railcraft Player Experience

A word of warning: If you plan to play Railcraft on Survival mode, you have a ton of work ahead of you. In Railcraft, you don't simply craft some rails and pop a minecart on them. Oh no—it's a much more complicated situation.

To that point, I'm going to "cheat" a bit and show you some stuff by using Creative mode so that we can immediately get our hands on all the Railcraft assets.

Log in to your Railcraft-enabled server from the client, making sure that your account is Opped.

Next, we'll set the gamemode to 1 (remember that 0 is Survival and 1 is Creative):

```
/gamemode 1
Set gamemode creative for [Player]TechTrainerTim
```

After we're in-world, find a nice mountainside as shown in Figure 6.10. We're going to use a tunnel bore (the coolest Minecraft asset you've ever seen!) to dig a 3×3 tunnel through that mountain and lay some minecart track!

FIGURE 6.10 The Railcraft tunnel bore will make (very) short work out of tunneling and laying minecart track through this mountain.

Open your inventory, because you're going to need quite a bit of stuff. First of all, navigate to page 2 of your inventory and click the crowbar—these are some of the Railcraft assets. Remember what I told you about mods fundamentally changing Minecraft? This is what I was talking about.

If you have a client-side mod like TooManyItems (discussed later in this chapter), you can simply type to search for the assets you need. You can see the TMI interface in Figure 6.11.

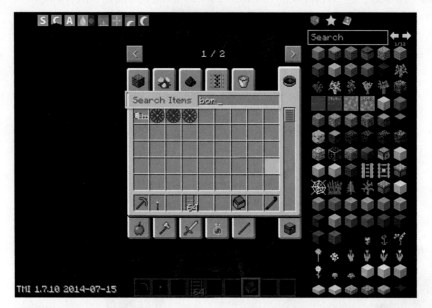

FIGURE 6.11   The TooManyItems client-side mod makes it easy to comb through the hundreds upon hundreds of default and Railcraft game assets.

To save time and space, let me give you a punch list of what you'll need in order to deploy a tunnel bore:

- Tunnel bore
- Diamond bore head
- Three to four full stacks of track (I like the reinforced track)
- Three to four full stacks of coal coke
- Three to four full stacks of gravel

TIP

Remember that in Creative mode you can Shift+click assets to transfer full stacks to your inventory.

We need to place at least one piece of track before we can place the tunnel bore. Be prepared for a surprise when you see the bore appear—it's huge!

Now lay down a few pieces of track behind the bore, and add a chest minecart. Using, your crowbar, Shift+right-click between the minecart and the bore to create a link, as shown in Figure 6.12.

The ability to create honest-to-goodness trains (and roller coasters) is a wonderful feature of Railcraft.

FIGURE 6.12 By linking one or more chest carts to your tunnel bore, you can catch all the blocks that the bore unearths. Here we see the tunnel bore already on its way.

We need to attach a drill bit and power the bore before it's functional. Walk alongside the bore and right-click the engine compartment. Figure 6.13 shows you the interface.

Here's what you do to power the tunnel bore:

- Add your diamond bore head to the Head block
- Add gravel to the Ballast blocks
- Add track to the Track block
- Add coal coke to the Fuel blocks

Make sure that you add the coal coke last because the bore has no on/off switch—it just goes as you can see in Figure 6.14.

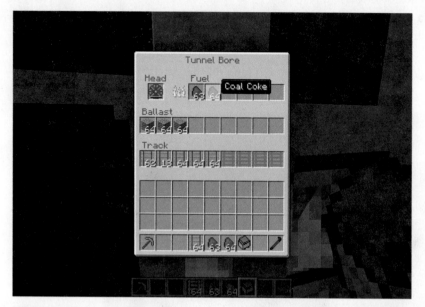

FIGURE 6.13 A Railcraft bore has several requirement performances that make it go.

FIGURE 6.14 Before long you'll have minecart tracks all over your world, with mountains being no object at all.

One more point about Railcraft's tunnel bore and then we'll move on: As long as you fill up the bore's ballast with gravel, the bore will compensate for any drops in elevation the best it can.

To test, I dug out ahead of the bore and made a pit. Check out Figure 6.15, in which you can see the bore dropping in granite.

FIGURE 6.15 The tunnel bore uses its gravel ballast blocks to fill in any potholes along the way.

CAUTION

Don't let the bore's drill bit touch you—it will badly hurt you.

Experimenting with Integrated Modpacks and Launchers

Over time, some Minecraft community development teams built such elaborate mods that it became cumbersome to get players into the game efficiently. To that point, nowadays we have several well-known modpacks that are essentially unified interfaces for a whole bunch of separate mods. Hence the term "modpack."

Feed the Beast (FTB)

The Feed the Best (affectionately called FTB; project page http://www.feed-the-beast.com/) platform is one of the most popular in today's Minecraft multiplayer universe. So much so, in fact, that many top-line Minecraft hosting providers support it.

In a nutshell, FTB is an end-to-end modpack solution. As you'll see in just a moment, the FTB custom launcher gives you complete control over which mods you want to play with; you can enable and disable at will. No more hunting around the Internet for the right file versions!

Go to the FTB Mod Packs page (http://www.feed-the-beast.com/mod-packs) and browse around. We'll use Direwolf20 for Minecraft v1.7.10 because this is a general-purpose mod-pack that includes every tech-oriented mod you can think of!

FOLLOW ME!

Getting Up and Running with FTB

In this brief exercise we'll download the FTB client and get it set up. Because I don't have access to my Macs as I type this, I'll conduct the tutorial under Windows 8.1.

1 Visit the project home page (http://www.feed-the-beast.com/) and click Download Now. Even though I'm on Windows, I'll choose Download (jar) to download the FTB launcher in `.jar` format.

2 Double-click the launcher and follow the prompts, accepting all defaults. The launcher will install to `c:\ftb` on Windows unless you override that.

3 The launcher's interface, shown in Figure 6.16, automates mod installation.

FIGURE 6.16   The Feed the Beast launcher. Here we've selected Direwolf20, one of the most popular general-purpose modpacks.

4 On the FTB Modpacks page, click Direwolf20 for Minecraft 1.7.10. Read through the modpack's contents in the right pane. Yes, indeed—Railcraft is on board.

5 In the lower right of the FTB launcher, open the drop-down menu and click Create Profile. Use your Minecraft account credentials here. When you're ready to rock, click Launch.

6 Go take a walk or pet your dog because it's going to take a while for FTB to download all those mods and get them installed.

7 After the Minecraft client appears, click Mods and wonder at how much more breadth and depth you added to the game. This is shown in Figure 6.17.

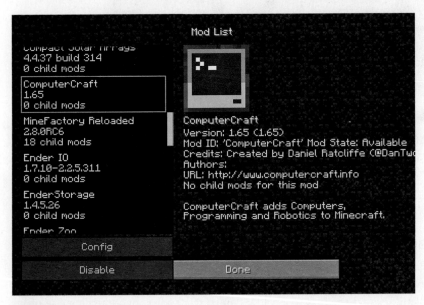

FIGURE 6.17 I find it overwhelming to have so many options available to me in Minecraft, but your mileage may vary.

8 Now get into the game and experiment! You'll need to perform a ton of research to learn how each mod works and how the mods can work together, but that's all part of the joy of Minecraft, am I correct? You can see a representative screenshot in Figure 6.18. That map in the upper-right is Rei's Minimap, which we'll discuss briefly at the end of this chapter.

FIGURE 6.18 After you get used to the FTB Minecraft environment, you'll probably never want to play "vanilla" ever again.

Installing FTB Server

Believe it or not, it's pretty straightforward setting up an FTB server. For instance, to download the Direwolf20 server, switch back to the FTB launcher, select the appropriate mod, and click the Download Server button.

The Direwolf server bits come to your computer as a compressed `.zip` archive. After the download completes, extract the files to a folder named `direwolf`, or something else of your choosing.

Edit either `ServerStart.bat` (Windows) or `ServerStart.sh` (OS X, Linux) to adjust the server's runtime properties. In Figure 6.19, for my Windows server, I didn't need to change anything.

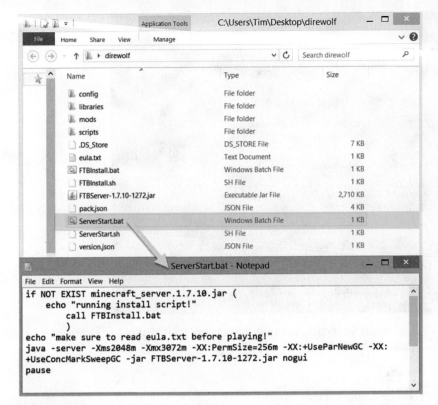

FIGURE 6.19 You should be familiar with analyzing and interpreting Minecraft server files by now. This is the Feed the Beast Direwolf20 server on a Windows 8.1 computer.

Start the FTB Direwolf server just like any other server we've dealt with over the course of the book. Yes, there's still the "first run, server halt, accept EULA" action. All connecting Minecraft clients need to download their own copy of the FTB launcher and start the proper modpack in order to connect to your server. You can see the unpleasant results of a failed client connection attempt (by using a non-FTB client) in Figure 6.20.

NOTE

In case you haven't figured this out yet, communication with your current and potential user base is a must, especially if your server has high entrance requirements such as an FTB server. We'll cover the so-called "soft skills" of Minecraft server administration later in this book.

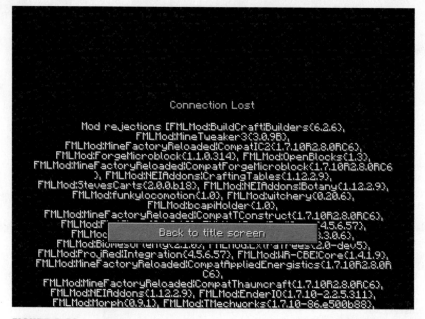

FIGURE 6.20 This is what your players see if they try to join your FTB server with a non-FTB Minecraft client.

Starting the FTB Launcher

Actually, I don't think it's obvious how to start the FTB launcher. Do you remember the `FTB_Launcher.jar` that we originally downloaded? That's what you use to start the launcher.

> **TIP**
>
> You might want to make a shortcut (Windows) or an alias (OS X) to that `.jar` on your desktop for easier use in the future.

ATLauncher and Other Options

ATLauncher (http://atlauncher.com) has some overlap with Feed the Beast, but they are separate products made by separate teams with separate goals.

I find the ATLauncher interface cleaner, easier to use, and more administrator friendly than the FTB launcher. On the other hand, I feel that FTB has a better lineup of modpacks. You can see the ATLauncher interface in Figure 6.21.

FIGURE 6.21 ATLauncher has a clean interface with some great server administrator features.

I will say this for ATLauncher, though: It's *fast*! Here a quick bullet list of some other modpack launchers for you to research and experiment with:

- TechnicPack: http://www.technicpack.net/
- Asterion Minecraft: http://asterionmc.com/robbit/
- GigaTech: http://minecraft-techworld.com/gigatech
- VoidLauncher: http://voidswrath.com/

Quality Client Mods

Not all Minecraft mods work on both servers and clients. Some mods are client-only. Consider making it as easy as possible for your players to download and install client mods to improve their gameplay if they aren't already using a modpack loader like FTB.

Here are some of what are generally considered the best Minecraft client mods:

Optifine (http://optifine.net/home): Greatly enhances game textures (shown in Figure 6.22).

Rei's Minimap (http://bit.ly/1ExL4Ow): Gives players an interactive map heads-up display (HUD) for simple navigation.

TooManyItems (http://bit.ly/1BnTneR): Inventory management and more.

FIGURE 6.22 Optifine improves the default game object textures—look at how crisp this panorama is.

The Bottom Line

You now have knowledge of all the required and suggested tools to host a dynamite Minecraft multiplayer server! I told you earlier in the book (a few times, actually) that hosting a server from your home isn't a good idea unless you need it for small LAN games.

The following two chapters solve that problem: By using a Minecraft multiplayer hosting service, we can apply all the cool new technologies and skills we've learned, and apply them in a truly scalable context.

"Our customers [for Realms] are parents who are tired of trying to act as server administrators on behalf of their kids."
–Carl Manneh, Mojang CEO

Exploring Minecraft Realms

What You'll Learn in This Chapter:

- Understanding cloud services
- Why Mojang created Realms
- How to join Realms and set up a realm
- How to play and manage Realms worlds

Alrighty, then! Prepare to learn some "real" IT in this chapter. To use the industry's language, thus far in the book we've concerned ourselves with "on-premises" Minecraft server deployments. In other words, our servers were hosted in all likelihood out of our home.

This chapter marks a fundamental shift in how we present our Minecraft server to the rest of the world. We'll learn how to use Mojang's own hosting solution, appropriately called Minecraft Realms.

By the end of this chapter, you'll be armed with all the knowledge you need to make an informed decision as to whether Realms is right for you.

Let's begin!

Understanding Cloud Services

As I said in the introduction, an on-premises service is a network service that is managed in its native environment. By the way, the term isn't "on premise," but "on premises." It appalls me how often I see people (including cloud hosting companies themselves) make this mistake. A premises is a location, while a premise is an idea. At any rate, on-premises Minecraft server deployments run into significant problems:

- Frequent outages (your server goes offline every time you restart or shut down your computer)
- Increased security risk (you're opening the door to your private internal network when you expose a Minecraft server to the Internet)
- Maintenance issues (you're responsible for all server and Minecraft "back-end" maintenance, including applying updates, backup, and restore)

By contrast, when you pay for a cloud-based hosting service such as Minecraft Realms, you get a lot more freedom (and fewer headaches overall) than you did as an on-premises server operator.

To see an illustration, take a look at the schematic diagram in Figure 7.1.

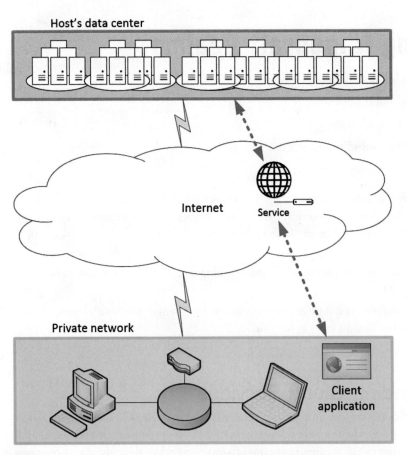

FIGURE 7.1 A bird's-eye perspective of public cloud services.

In a public cloud scenario, the end user (also called the service subscriber) interacts with an Internet-based service by using some client application. In the case of Minecraft, naturally, that client application is the Minecraft client.

The end user knows absolutely nothing about the actual server or servers that host that resource; that's not what you're paying for. Behind the veil of the cloud, the host manages all the back-end mechanics of keeping the service available and backed up.

In fact, that's why we use the metaphor of the cloud: The end user never sees what's "behind the cloud," as it were, in terms of actual data center/server technology.

The "public" in the phrase "public cloud" means that the hosting provider makes the service available at a cost to multiple subscribers.

Pros and Cons

As with just about any choice in life, much less just with technology, there exist pros, cons, and trade-offs that you make when you decide to pay for a cloud service rather than host the service yourself. I've summarized the major points in Table 7.1.

TABLE 7.1 Public Cloud Service Advantages and Disadvantages

Advantage	Disadvantage
You don't have to worry about day-to-day server maintenance	You have less administrative flexibility
The service scales to meet user demand	Your subscription might have service limits, with extra money for overages
You have great service uptime	There's the question of data sovereignty—who owns your service data?

The data in Table 7.1 will become increasingly clear to you as we proceed through our exploration of Minecraft Realms.

Introducing Minecraft Realms

Minecraft Realms is Mojang's own hosted public cloud service. For a flat monthly fee, Mojang provides you with up to three highly available worlds in a white-listed environment, although only one can be active at a time.

In a curious twist, you get a minigame world in addition to the three full ones. I think the reason Mojang gave us Realms in general, and the minigames in particular, is to give Minecraft fans an official way to play Minecraft. Remember, after all, that most of the unofficial servers have been stricken with licensing issues and tend toward being unpredictable at best and unstable at worst.

You invite players to give them access to your world, and your multiplayer game can host up to 10 simultaneous users. According to Mojang, realm operators have access to "most" console commands, although mods or plugins of any kind are not allowed.

One more thing you should know before we sign up for Realms: The online worlds all run the latest public Minecraft release, so you'll need to have a premium account and run the latest launcher and latest game version. It goes without saying (although here I am saying it anyway) that you shouldn't bother with Realms if you're using a cracked launcher with or without a fake Minecraft account.

Let's Sign Up!

To get started, go to http://minecraft.net and log in with your Minecraft account. I've found that it helps to sign in before signing up for Realms.

Next, point your web browser to the Minecraft Realms home page (http://minecraft.net/realms), shown in Figure 7.2. As you can see in the figure, a Realms subscriptions costs $13 per month as of this writing. Click Get Realms to continue.

FIGURE 7.2 The Minecraft Realms home page.

On the Buy Realms Subscription page, shown in Figure 7.3, you can choose to subscribe in one-, three-, or six-month blocks (payable in a one-time charge and with a discount), or one month at a time with auto-extension enabled.

NOTE

I've found Mojang to be very fair in their licensing; you can cancel your recurring subscription at any time. Although I haven't done it, I'd bet that Mojang would prorate your cancellation if you used a prepaid plan instead.

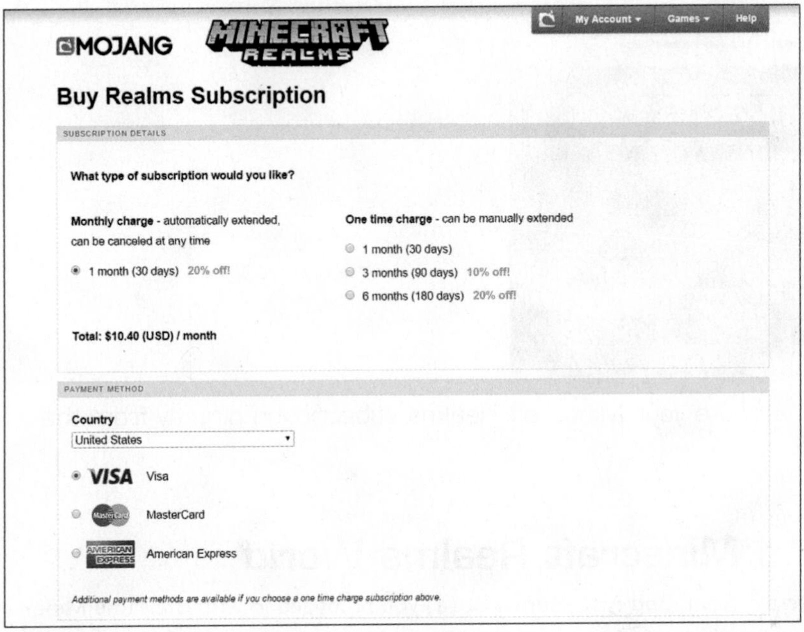

FIGURE 7.3 Mojang gives us flexibility (and no long-term subscription commitment) for their Realms service.

You can pay for your Realms subscription either with a credit card or with PayPal.

After your payment is processed, you'll be given your receipt (see Figure 7.4) and some instructions on how to access your newly activated subscription.

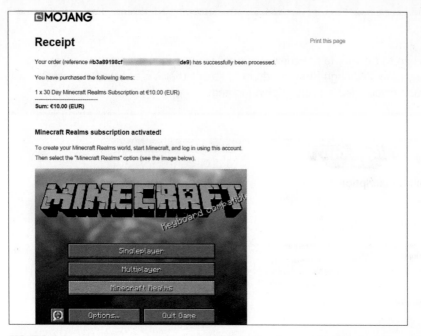

FIGURE 7.4 You activate your Minecraft Realms subscription directly from the Minecraft client.

Playing in a Minecraft Realms World

Fire up your Minecraft client, and make sure that (a) you're logged in with the same Minecraft account you used when you purchased your Realms subscription; and (b) you're running the latest version of the game.

I show you the profile editor in Figure 7.5 for your reference, although I'm almost positive I don't have to. After all, you're probably an expert in Minecraft profile management, given the different game versions and Forge additions we've made to the game in the book thus far.

As shown in Figure 7.6, we'll use the Minecraft Realms button to access our Realms subscription.

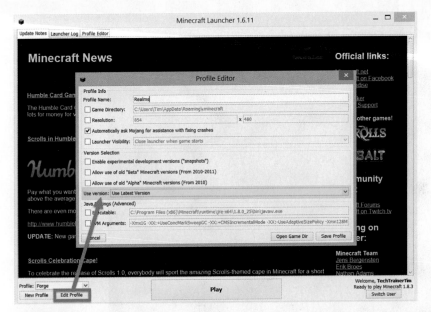

FIGURE 7.5 Minecraft Realms requires that you're running the latest Minecraft public release.

FIGURE 7.6 Although you might have ignored the Minecraft Realms button thus far, now it's central to our game experience.

As long as you're logged in to the appropriate Minecraft account, you'll see the Click to Create Realm button, as shown in Figure 7.7. Click that button to proceed.

FIGURE 7.7 As you can see, Minecraft Realms has its own administrative interface.

After accepting the terms of service, you'll be asked to give the realm a name and, optionally, to select a starter template. Let's click Select Template to open the Realm Templates screen (see Figure 7.8).

When you return to the Minecraft Realms home page, you'll see your newly created realm appear along with a couple of important status icons (see Figure 7.9).

FIGURE 7.8 Community-submitted world templates give you a head start on building an interesting multiplayer world.

FIGURE 7.9 Most pretty icons on this page actually perform an action. The envelope icon, for instance, records pending invitations.

Inviting Players

In the Minecraft Realms page, select your new realm and then click Configure. We're going to invite our zoey2010 test player to join our realm. The Configure Realm screen appears, as shown in Figure 7.10.

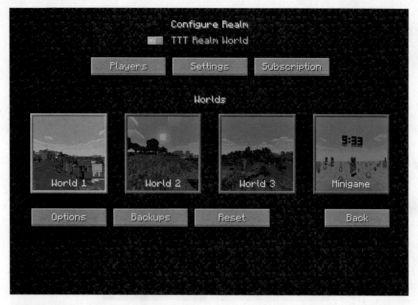

FIGURE 7.10 Your Minecraft Realms subscription gives you three "full" worlds and one minigame world. However, only one world can be active at a time.

Click Players to switch focus to the Players screen, and then click Invite player. Fill in the player's Minecraft username (zoey2010 in my case), and then click Invite Player. You'll now see the player appear in the Invited list, as shown in Figure 7.11.

FIGURE 7.11 The Players screen gives us complete control over our realm's whitelist.

Now, as Zoey, we'll fire up another Minecraft client and click Minecraft Realms on the home page. As you can see in Figure 7.12, the envelope icon is "lit up" with a pending invitation notification.

FIGURE 7.12 Cool—we've been invited to join as a player in someone's Minecraft Realms server!

Zoey will then see TechTrainerTim's Realm in the list; let's click Accept to confirm the invitation (see Figure 7.13).

FIGURE 7.13 Your players need to accept your invitation before they can play on your Minecraft Realms server.

Now we're cooking with gas. Finally, Zoey selects the TTT Realm World and then clicks Play to join the game. Note the status icon that appears to the right of the realm name; the icon appears in one of three colors:

- Green: online
- Gray: offline
- Red: expired (closed subscription)

Managing Players

The actual gameplay in Minecraft Realms is essentially the same as with any vanilla Minecraft server, with the exception that (a) you can have a maximum of 10 players in the world; and (b) you don't have access to all server console commands.

As a quick review, here are some of the basic commands I tend to use a lot in Realms multiplayer:

/time set day 1000: Especially when I'm experimenting, I like my world to have the sun shining all the time. Keeps the monsters away as well.

/gamerule doDaylightCycle false: This keeps the time constant all the time—it's like Las Vegas, but without the gambling!

/toggledownfall: Makes rain go away almost instantly.

/setworldspawn: As an OP, you determine the entry point to your world. We'll have a lot more to say about world spawn points in a future chapter.

/list: See who is on your server right now.

/summon: Add some spice to the game by invoking mobs, hostile or otherwise, into your world.

NOTE

You might see references to Minecraft SMP in your Internet travels. SMP stands for "Survival Multiplayer," which happens to be the most common Minecraft multiplayer scenario. So now you know.

You'll be (un)pleasantly surprised when you run into unsupported Minecraft server commands. For instance, if I want to OP zoey2010, the following command fails with this error:

```
/op zoey2010
You do not have permission to use this command.
```

As it happens, you manage your players through the Realms GUI interface. Disconnect from your game, return to the Configure screen, and click Players. Toggle the player's role (Normal User or Operator) by clicking the icon next to the player's name, as shown in Figure 7.14.

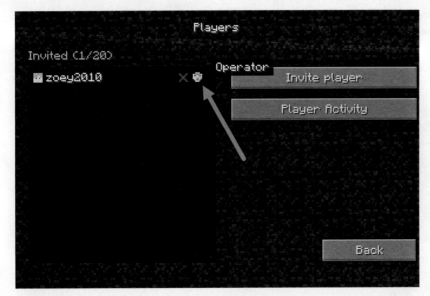

FIGURE 7.14 You OP and de-OP Realms players by using the GUI interface.

Another strange Realms behavior I found was that I couldn't use /kick to remove players from a game session. These are your two options for doing something like this:

- Close your world.
- Remove the player from your whitelist.

Toggle the on/off switch for your world (see Figure 7.15) to close the Realms server. When you do this, any connected players get kicked. That's shown in Figure 7.15 as well.

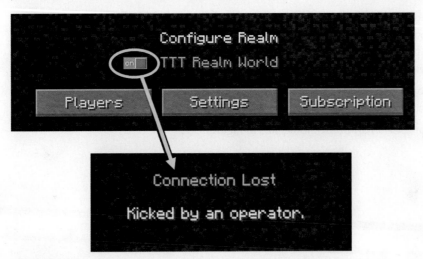

FIGURE 7.15 When you shut off a Realms server (top), all connected players are kicked (bottom).

Of course, closing the server kicks *everyone* from the server rather than an individual user. Head over to the Players screen and click the X icon to remove a player from your whitelist (see Figure 7.16). The problem with uninviting players, of course, is that you'll have to reinvite them if you want them to return to your Realms server someday.

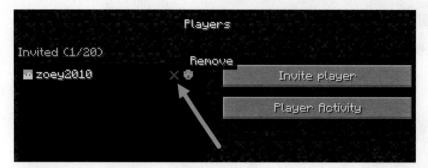

FIGURE 7.16 You can't precisely kick a player in Realms, but you can remove a player from the whitelist.

I hope that Mojang/Microsoft revamps Realms to make the experience easier to use and more convenient both for operators and players.

A Brief Tutorial on Command Blocks

A command block is a special kind of block that stores Minecraft console commands. From a single-player Survival game with cheats enabled, you can give yourself a command block with the /give command:

```
/give TechTrainerTim command_block 1
```

Command blocks are especially important in a multiplayer world because we can inject console code into our players' game experience. For example, we could have a command block that teleports a player to another world on our server, or back to the world spawn point, or to another location on the map.

We might use command blocks to give players equipment or food. We can use them to change the weather, blow up TNT—whatever strikes our fancy.

You can see what a command block looks like in Figure 7.17.

FIGURE 7.17 Command blocks are often the "secret sauce" that separates an ordinary Minecraft server from an exceptional one.

About Target Selectors

Before you can be effective with command blocks in Minecraft, you need to understand target selectors. Let me share the codes with you first, and then you'll learn how to use them:

- **@p:** Targets the nearest player.
- **@r:** Targets a random player.
- **@a:** Targets all players, including dead ones!
- **@e:** Targets all entities, including players.

Let's say you used F3 to get your current coordinates (x=104, y=71, z=33, for the sake of example), and you want to teleport all connected players to that location. Here's how you'd construct your teleport command by using the @a target selector:

```
/tp @a 104 71 33
```

Or perhaps you want to strike down a random player in your multiplayer map (you meanie, you!):

```
/kill @r
```

You'll see in a moment how we can use target selectors in a very powerful way by using them to program command blocks.

Programming Command Blocks

It's time to practice our Minecraft console coding. After all, I strongly hold that teachers can use Minecraft as a platform to teach kids of all ages how to do not only server administration but also programming.

FOLLOW ME!

Working with Command Blocks

In this exercise we'll create a command block that gives the closest player one stone pickaxe (we don't want to make the game too easy for our players, do we?).

Make sure you're logged in to your Realms Survival world as an operator.

1 We can give ourselves, but not program, command blocks in Survival mode:

```
/give TechTrainerTim command_block 1
```

2 Find a cool spot on your map for your "gift" command block, and set it down. We'll need to shift our game mode to creative for a moment:

```
/gamemode 1
```

3 Right-click the command block to open the Set Console Command for Block interface, shown in Figure 7.18.

FIGURE 7.18 After you test the power of command blocks, you'll likely use them all the time in your Minecraft multiplayer maps.

4 We know how to use the `/give` command; let's modify it by using the `@p` selector:

```
/give @p stone_pickaxe 1
```

The Previous Output box shows you whether the last command block use resulted in success or failure. This information can be helpful for debugging purposes. Right now, however, nobody has activated the command block, so we have no output. Click Done to continue.

5 Command blocks require a redstone signal in order to work. To set that up, let's switch the game mode back to Survival and give ourselves redstone and a lever:

```
/gamemode 0
/give TechTrainerTim redstone 10
/give TechTrainerTim lever 1
```

6 Now lay a stripe of redstone dust over the block; I need to apply the dust to three sides, as shown in Figure 7.19.

FIGURE 7.19 Our friendly free stone shovel station.

7 Finally, add your lever as an activator, and you're done.

8 To test, walk up to the lever and flip the switch. Voilá! Now clear your inventory and test again:

```
/clear
```

Configuring Minecraft Realms

Let's spend the remainder of this chapter on how to "care for" our Minecraft Realms worlds. We'll begin with the crucial concept of backup and restore.

Backup and Restore

Joining an online Minecraft server is a trust issue. Do I trust, for instance, that the server operator takes steps to minimize the possibility of data loss?

What if I invested 40 hours in participating in an awesome build, only to log in tomorrow and see that the world's gone? That's not a good thing, and your rep as a server operator will suffer if this happens to you.

Viewing Backups

From the Realms home page in the Minecraft client, select your realm and click Configure. Next, select your world (remember that you get three with your subscription) and click Backups. I am flummoxed as to Mojang's backup schedule for Realms. As you can see in Figure 7.20, you get more than one backup per day. However, the specific algorithm used is unknown to the best of my knowledge.

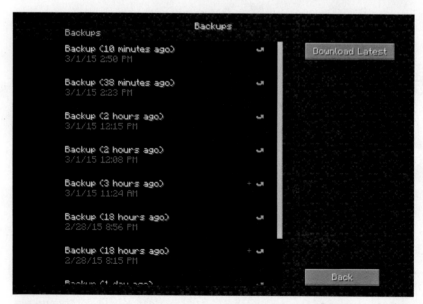

FIGURE 7.20 The Minecraft Realms backup and restore interface.

Forcing a Backup

As enjoyable as the Minigame world is in Realms, it has a more important function to me as a Realms administrator. As it happens, you can force Mojang to back up your current world by switching to the Minigame, and then back to your original world. Here's the procedure:

1 On the Configure Realm page, click the Minigame.

2 On the Switch Realm to Mini Game page, choose a minigame from the list and click Switch.

3 Return to the Configure Realm page and switch back to your original world.

4 Go to the Backups page for your world and notice the most recent backup. Score!

Downloading a World to Single-Player

Navigate back to the Backups page for your chosen Realms world. Next, click Download Latest. Realms will ask you to confirm that you want to download the latest backup of your world to the single-player game.

From the Backups page, click Download Latest. A page appears, letting you know that the active world will be downloaded and added to your single-player worlds. Click Yes to continue, and wait a while for your Realms world to be copied (not moved) to your single-player game.

From the Minecraft client home page, click Singleplayer. Double-click your downloaded world (mine is shown in Figure 7.21) to join in single-player mode.

FIGURE 7.21 I brought down a copy of one of my Realms worlds to my single-player game.

TIP

One suggestion for using the Realms download/upload functionality is to give you some "breathing room" when making major world modifications. For example, you can download a copy of your world, customize it to your heart's content without relying on an Internet connection and with no other players interrupting, and upload your finished product back to Realms. Clean and easy.

Uploading a World to Realms

By contrast, you can upload any of your single-player Minecraft worlds to Realms. For instance, I created a superflat Creative mode world in single-player, and I now want to share it with my friends through Realms. Here's how it works:

1 Log in to Realms and navigate to the Configure page for your active world.

2 Click Reset—and no, I'm not kidding. This pathway to do a world upload is unfortunate in my humble opinion.

3 In the Reset World dialog, shown in Figure 7.22, click Upload World, and then select your single-player world and click Upload.

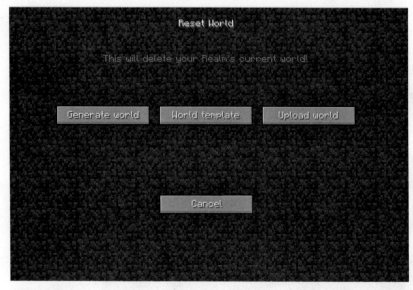

FIGURE 7.22 Why Mojang hid the Upload function in the Reset World page I might never understand.

Be aware that you just overwrote your currently active world with the one from your single-player environment! To ward against this problem from occurring in the future, perform one of the following actions:

- Switch to another of your three worlds and overwrite that one with your single-player world.

- Perform a restore of your original Realms world.

One more thing: In my experience I have to restart the Minecraft client in order to log in to my newly uploaded world. You might also need to wait a few minutes for the "dust to settle" on Mojang's side before attempting a reconnection.

Restoring a World

To restore a previously saved snapshot of your selected world, navigate back to the Backups page, locate an appropriate snapshot, and click the arrow button that appears to the right of the backup name.

You'll be prompted to confirm your action, and if you click Yes, the world will be restored within mere seconds.

I can't stress how important and convenient the backup/restore functionality is to Minecraft server. The Realms service totally automates the process, which is great.

The Bottom Line

As Mojang CEO Carl Manneh said in the chapter's opening quote, this service does indeed provide a clean and easy way for kids (of all ages) to host a Minecraft server. Moreover, you don't have to worry about the vast majority of administration tasks that you do if you're managing a LAN server.

On the other hand, the fact is that Realms is frustratingly limited to

- Ten-player maximum

- Whitelist only

- No mods or plugins

- Partial console command set

This means that Realms simply isn't a possibility for many potential Minecraft server operators. The good news for you is that in the next chapter we'll learn how to use Minecraft hosts that have none of the aforementioned restrictions. Are you excited? Let's get to it!

8

> "Only you can control your future."
> —Dr. Seuss

Taking Control of Minecraft with Third-Party Hosting

What You'll Learn in This Chapter:

- How to find the right Minecraft host
- Deep-diving into MCProHosting
- Configuring, running, and tweaking your server
- Locating other reputable Minecraft hosts

We've come a long way thus far, haven't we? By now you understand how to host your own Minecraft server and the security risks involved with that.

You also understand how Mojang's Minecraft Realms service works with its inherent limitations.

In this chapter, I'm excited to present to you the best of both worlds. By using a third-party Minecraft hosting service, you can have the convenience and power of a cloud-based host, but also most of the flexibility that comes with owning your own server.

We'll begin our discussion by covering the two big questions that most newcomers have regarding this topic:

- What do all the funky terms such as "VPS" mean?
- What do I look for in a Minecraft host?

Let's get to work.

What to Look for in a Third-Party Minecraft Host

Actually, before we get to the characteristics that separate quality Minecraft hosting companies from ones to be avoided, we should cover the basic vocabulary so that we know our terms.

Minecraft Hosting Terminology

If you read the preceding chapter, you know what a "cloud hosting provider" is. In this case, the hosting provider sells their computing power to you for the purpose of running online Minecraft multiplayer games.

Take a look at Figure 8.1, in which I compare VPS versus dedicated Minecraft hosting.

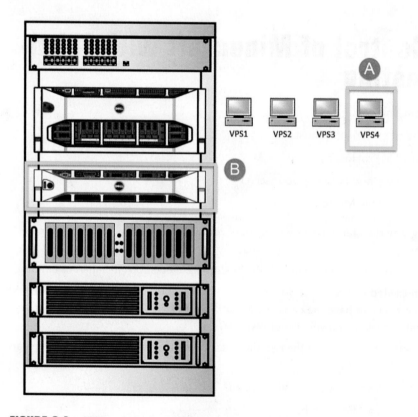

FIGURE 8.1 Differentiating VPS versus dedicated Minecraft server hosting from the computer hardware perspective.

A *virtual private server*, or *VPS*, is shared computing power. Physically, this means that your subscription pays for a virtual machine (VM) that runs along with several other VMs on the same physical rack server in the hosting company's data centers. You can look at a VM as a software-based "computer inside a computer"; the hosting company allocates physical hardware resources (processor, memory, disk storage, and network bandwidth) to the VMs in a controlled manner. The more you pay, the more computing power your VM is allotted.

The VPS approach is certainly more cost-effective than buying a *dedicated* Minecraft server. At least on paper, you're paying for an entire physical server located in your host's data centers.

I'm skeptical that most Minecraft hosts actually reserve an entire physical box for you when you pay for a "dedicated" server. More likely, you're still paying for a VPS, but with increased allocations for processor, memory, disk, and network resources.

The cost difference between VPS and dedicated servers is significant, and unless you already have a superpopular Minecraft server, I strongly suggest you go with VPS.

What's Important in a Minecraft Host

Do not underestimate the power of word of mouth. If one of your friends had a good relationship with a Minecraft hosting service, you should take that information under advisement.

If you don't know what you're doing, you can get ripped off because unethical business-people know how popular Minecraft is, and how ignorant most people are concerning stuff such as server hardware and networking concepts.

Thus, *reputation* is important. For example, I chose to use MCProHosting as our case study Minecraft host because they are top-rated and I personally had a great experience with them as a customer.

Your Minecraft host should publish their *server specifications* on their website. Those that don't should be considered suspect. For example, here's what MCProHosting publishes on their website: "We utilize Dual Xeon E5-2620 Processors, DDR3 ECC RAM, Samsung SSDs, and 1Gbps blended fiber connections on each box."

That's a lot of tech-speak, but what does it actually mean? First of all, Minecraft is a single-threaded application, which means that it can access only one central processing unit (CPU) core at a time. Thus, don't worry about "Dual" or multicore CPU references. DD3 ECC RAM is standard, but you pay for that when you choose your plan. The "Samsung SSD" reference means that MC uses solid-state drives, which is a big deal.

In a nutshell, SSD hard drives are faster than traditional hard drives because SSDs have no moving parts. Finally, the "1Gbps blended fiber connection" tells us that MC has a fast network connection. What this isn't telling us, however, is whether that 1Gbps is upload or download speed.

In a Minecraft server, upload speed is typically more important because the server needs to constantly send graphics data to your players.

Long story short: You can geek out on hardware benchmarking, but here are my recommendations:

CPU: Don't worry about multicores, but higher speed numbers mean better server performance (in general).

RAM: The speed of the RAM chips is moderately important, but not as important as the net RAM amount you get with your plan.

Disk: SSD storage is definitely recommended over hard disk drive (HDD) storage.

Network: Faster is obviously better, but try to find out separate numbers for upload/download.

Another aspect that should guide your Minecraft hosting company selection is *availability*. This metric means (a) what uptime percentage the provider guarantees, and (b) whether the provider has multiple points of presence (POP).

For example, MCProHosting has data centers located in the following cities:

- Phoenix, Arizona
- Ashburn, Virginia
- Amsterdam, Netherlands (perfect for all around E.U.)
- Dallas, Texas (great for all around U.S.)
- San Jose, California
- Seattle, Washington
- Singapore, Asia (low ping in Australia)
- Hong Kong, China

This is a good thing because having multiple data centers means that (a) your players get better play speeds because they'll be directed to their nearest server, and (b) your server stays online because it's being mirrored across multiple sites.

Finally, we have the question of *flexibility*. We need a service that will allow us to mod our server with Bukkit, Spigot, Feed the Beast, or some combination thereof.

Not all Minecraft hosts support third-party servers!

Along the same lines, what kind of access does the hosting provider give you to your server? Many companies use a Web-based control panel, such as Multicraft (http://www.multicraft.org/), whereas others give you File Transfer Protocol (FTP) and Secure Shell (SSH) command-line access to the server itself. The latter method is more typical in dedicated hosting environments. With VPS, you'll probably use a Web-based control panel.

To recap: In scouting out a quality Minecraft hosting service, get answers to your questions concerning the following:

- Reputation
- Server specifications

- Availability
- Flexibility

NOTE

Please know that I was not paid or given any special treatment by MCProHosting. I chose to include them in this book because they came up in my research as a top hosting company, and I personally had a good experience with them as a customer. Feel free to do your own research.

Joining MCProHosting

If you feel so inspired, point your web browser to MCProHosting and let me walk you through the process of signing up for Minecraft hosting service.

Our first task is to choose a plan. The MCProHosting plan matrix (https://mcprohosting. com/plans#/name?plans=mc, shown in Figure 8.2) cleverly employs Minecraft ore types to denote their service levels.

FIGURE 8.2 MCProHosting uses Minecraft ores to denote different service-plan levels.

The general guideline is that your Minecraft server should reserve 100 megabytes (MB) per user. Thus, I'll choose the Stone plan, which gives us 1 gigabyte (GB) RAM, which averages out to about 10 concurrent players. MC says 25, but I won't argue.

You're then asked to log in with your Minecraft username, after which you choose your preferred game type (see Figure 8.3).

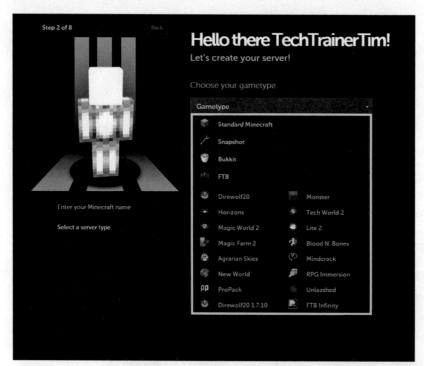

FIGURE 8.3 MCProHosting enables us to run some of the most popular Minecraft server mods on the Internet, including Feed the Beast Direwolf20.

I'll choose Bukkit here and continue. We're next asked to specify our expected number of players and the nearest geographic location (see Figure 8.4).

Next, we choose a map for our shared world (see Figure 8.5). MC offers a nice variety of maps; I'll choose Homestead and continue.

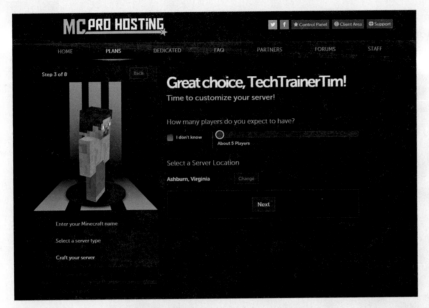

FIGURE 8.4 MCProHosting optimizes your VPS based on the information you supply concerning player population and your geographical location.

FIGURE 8.5 A good Minecraft hosting service offers customers an excellent selection of world maps.

Easy does it—don't freak out if you see options as displayed in Figure 8.6. You can always make configuration changes after you complete the account registration process; here we're asked to specify initial values.

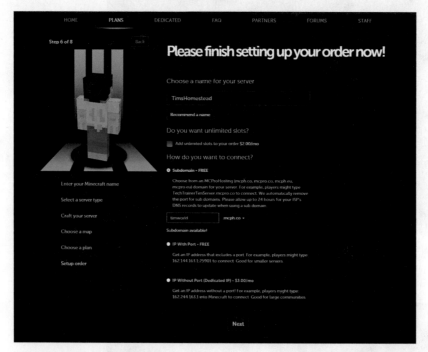

FIGURE 8.6   Don't worry about making the "wrong choice" when you set up your account; you can always edit your settings later.

With regard to MCProHosting's "initial values," here's what's going on:

Unlimited slots: This option allows you to adjust the maximum number of simultaneous players on your VPC.

Subdomain: This option allows you to give your players an easy-to-remember name instead of an IP address/port number combination.

IP with Port: This option requires that you provide the IP address and nonstandard port number to your players.

Dedicated IP: This option reserves a public IP address for you and advertises your server on the Minecraft default port (25565).

One thing that annoys me about many service providers, MCProHosting included, is the "upsell" enticements that you need to wade through when signing up for service. Take a look at Figure 8.7 to see what I mean.

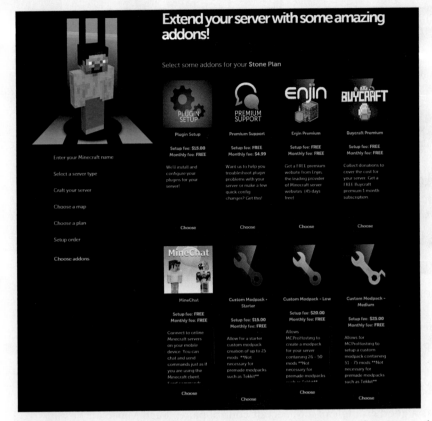

FIGURE 8.7 One common way that service providers make money is to entice you with upsell service add-ons. These are optional.

Of course, it's up to you which of these add-ons, if any, you add to your order. Again, you'll have ample time and opportunity to add them to your plan later, so don't feel pressured here. For my part, I'll pass and click Next.

The rest of the MCProHosting registration process is straightforward. Here's what I did:

- Provided my contact information
- Created a username and password
- Provided my credit card information

You can watch your VPC being built before your eyes (see Figure 8.8).

FIGURE 8.8 Here we're watching MCProHosting provision our Minecraft server.

You'll receive a few email messages from the host that confirm payment and give you a link to your control panel. Speaking of control panels, that's what we'll learn how to use next.

Getting to Know the Control Panel

McMyAdmin was a good example of a Minecraft control panel. Each Minecraft hosting provider has their own approach to letting their customers manage their servers; MCPro-Hosting uses a modified version of the Multicraft control panel.

You probably notice by scanning the MCProHosting website that nearly every page has a Control Panel button; use this to access your account.

After you're logged in to the control panel, you're taken to the My Server page, as shown in Figure 8.9.

Across the top of the control panel interface you see four tabs:

My Server: Configure your VPS.

Billing: Edit your payment information.

Profile: Change your password.

Logout: Leave the control panel.

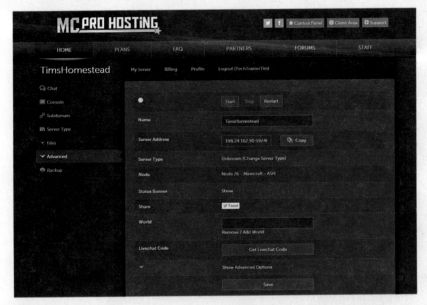

FIGURE 8.9 MCProHosting uses a modified version of the Multicraft control panel.

Along the left, you see a navigation menu with the following options:

Chat: Send messages to connected players (messages appear in the Minecraft client).

Console: See a web-based version of the Minecraft server console.

Subdomain: Manage your server's subdomain name.

Server Type: Customize the server type (vanilla versus Bukkit versus FTB, and so forth).

Files: Load a world, access config files, install plugins, and gain FTP access.

Advanced: Manage user accounts, players, commands, scheduled tasks, and MySQL databases.

Backup: Manage server backups and adjust your disk space quota.

Configuring and Starting Our Minecraft Server

Let's navigate to the Server Type page and customize the kind of Minecraft server we're operating. Check out Figure 8.10; after I choose Bukkit as my server type, I select a compatible Minecraft version, and then optionally rename my .jar file.

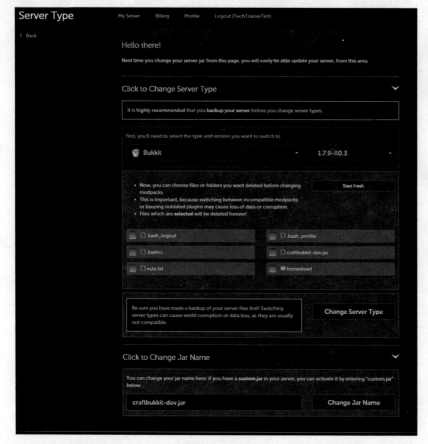

FIGURE 8.10 Customizing our Minecraft server type.

Now go back to the My Server page and click Start to boot your virtual server. We're on our way now!

Logging In

I'll start my Minecraft client, making sure to edit my profile (My Bukkit server runs v1.7.9). With MCProHosting, we have two connection options:

- Subdomain
- IP address/port

It makes no sense to use the second option when MCProHosting gives us an easy-to-remember server name. In the control panel, go to the Subdomains page to verify the address. After you're in the Minecraft client, add the new multiplayer server by name, as shown in Figure 8.11.

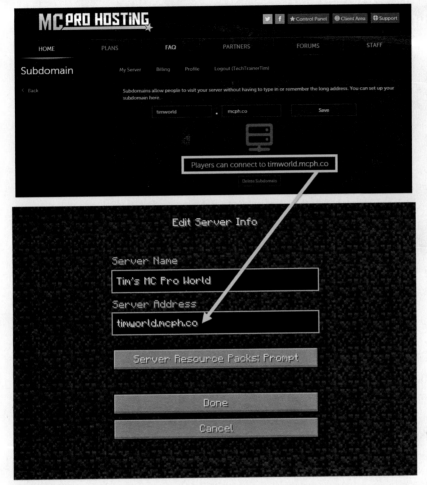

FIGURE 8.11 Using a subdomain from our hosting company makes it easier for players to join your world.

You'll find that your account has regular player privileges in your world. You'll also discover that you can't OP yourself from within the Minecraft client.

Instead, switch back to control panel, navigate to the console, and issue the following command:

```
op TechTrainerTim
```

The web-based Minecraft server console is shown in Figure 8.12.

FIGURE 8.12   You should do most of your world administration from the web console.

Adding Some Plugins

As we know, a Bukkit server is a modded Minecraft server, but we don't add tangible value to our players until we load some plugins.

In control panel, open the Files navigation drop-down, and then click BukGet Plugins. Buk-Get (https://bukget.org/) is an API that automates Bukkit plugin installation.

The BukGet integration in the MCProHosting control panel is first-class. No more cruising around the Web and negotiating AdFly pages to find your favorite Bukkit plugins!

FOLLOW ME!

Installing a Plugin on our Hosted Server

In this exercise we'll install the Essentials plugin on our MCProHosting VPS.

1   From control panel, navigate to the BukGet Plugin List. Open the Categories drop-down to see the varieties of Bukkit plugins that are available. These include the following (as of this writing):

Admin Tools

Anti-Griefing Tools

Chat-Related

Client Fun

Client Teleportation

Developer Tools

Economy

Fixes

Fun

General

Informational

Mechanics

Miscellaneous

Role-Playing

Teleportation

Website Administration

World Editing and Management

World Generators

2 Alternatively, type `Essentials` into the Plugin Name search field and press Enter or Return to find matches. In the results list, click Essentials.

3 On the Essentials page, click Install. The preceding step and this one are shown in Figure 8.13.

4 Return to the My Server page and click Restart to reboot your server.

5 Log in to the game and verify that Essentials is working. You should see "You have no new mail" in the chat window if it is.

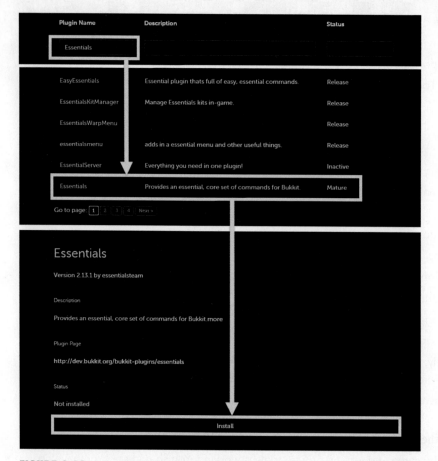

FIGURE 8.13   The BukGet API simplifies the discovery and installation of Bukkit plugins.

The Chat functionality with MCProHosting is pretty cool. In control panel, click Chat, type a message, and click Send. As you can see in Figure 8.14, observe that you can also kick players through this interface.

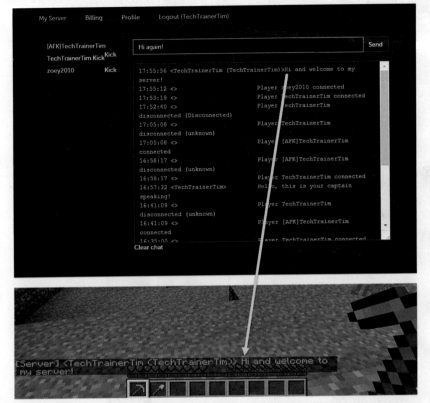

FIGURE 8.14 The chat console allows us to blast out messages to all connected players. Notice that we can also use the GUI to kick players.

Making Additional Tweaks to Your Server

The tasks that I'm teaching you in this chapter apply to *any* full-featured Minecraft hosting service, not just MC. In fact, you're likely to use the Multicraft control panel in another hosting environment.

Editing Your Config Files

We've grown accustomed, I think, to making changes to our LAN server's .yml configuration files. We do this because, in the last analysis, this is how we tweak our Minecraft server!

In control panel, use the left-hand navigation bar and click Files, Config Files, as shown in Figure 8.15.

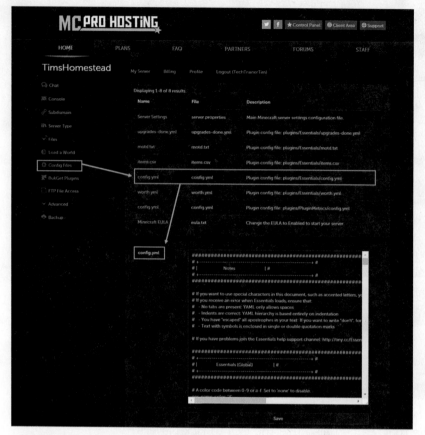

FIGURE 8.15 We edit our Minecraft server config files directly in the browser.

Click one of the config files (in Figure 8.15 I chose `config.yml`, the main Essentials config file). You'll see the file open directly in the browser, where you're free to edit it as you see fit. Two things to remember when you're finished editing:

1 Click Save Your Changes.

2 Restart your server from the My Server page.

In control panel, click Files, FTP File Access to see the full file system of your VPS. To be more technically correct, you can't see the full file system of your virtual server, but instead all the contents of your Minecraft server installation folder, as shown in Figure 8.16.

FIGURE 8.16 With MCProHosting, even FTP access to your files occurs in the context of the Web control panel.

Deploying a Resource Pack

You probably already use resource packs to customize the look and feel of Minecraft world assets in the single-player game. Did you know that you can deploy resource packs on your Minecraft server? Even better, MCProHosting has a feature in which we can "automagically" deploy resource packs to incoming players.

Let's deploy the famous Faithful 32x32 resource pack. I like this one because it maintains the classic Minecraft look and feel, but doubles the display resolution, resulting in ultra-sharp textures.

CAUTION

Be sure to download Faithful 32x32 for your correct Minecraft version!

Use your search engine skills to locate the proper version of Faithful 32x32 and download the .zip file.

We're going to need to upload the .zip to a cloud file-sharing service before we can add it to our MCProHosting server account. I use Dropbox (http://dropbox.com), so I'll use that platform as an example.

As you'll observe in Figure 8.17, I logged in to my Dropbox account and uploaded the `faithful32pack.zip` file to my personal "cloud."

FIGURE 8.17   If you're not already using a cloud-based file hosting service like Dropbox, you should be!

In Dropbox we can share the `.zip` file simply by selecting the archive and clicking Share. As shown in Figure 8.18, we need to copy the link to that cloud-based asset; this is the address that MCProHosting needs.

> **Share link to 'faithful32pack.zip'**   ✕
>
> Link to file
>
> `https://www.dropbox.com/s/fvtkklwmd046tte/faithful32pack.zip?dl=0`
>
> ⟳ Anyone with the link can see it. Set visibility / expiration
>
> Send this link to
>
> Email or name
>
> Message (optional)
>
> **Send**   **Close**

FIGURE 8.18   We need to retrieve the sharing address for our resource pack before we can deploy it to our Minecraft server.

Back in control panel, we'll click Files, Config Files, and then click Server Settings to open `server.properties` in the browser. Find the Resource Pack (Link to .zip) field and paste in your shared file link from the earlier steps. The screen is shown in Figure 8.19.

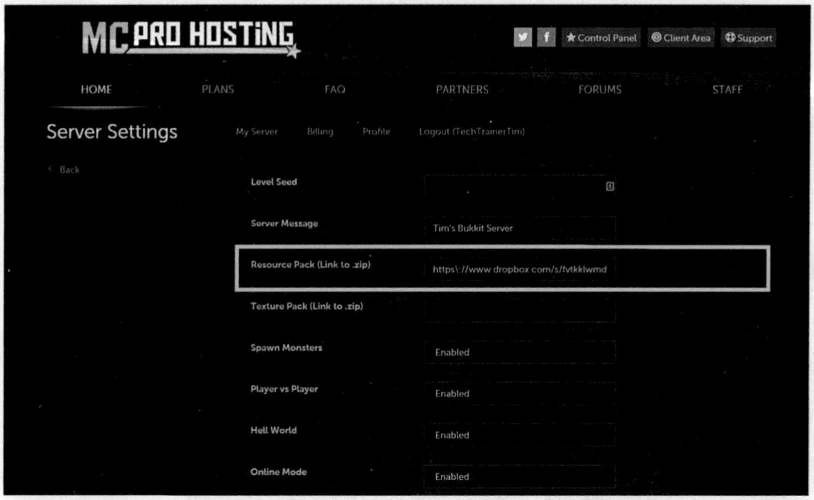

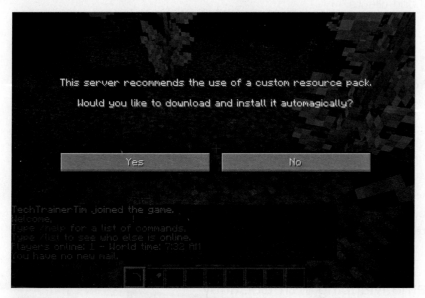

FIGURE 8.19   Adding a resource pack to our hosted Minecraft server.

Click Save to save your changes. To be safe, restart your Minecraft server before testing with a Minecraft client.

Upon first connection to your server, the player will be prompted to automagically download and install the resource pack from the server, as shown in Figure 8.20. Pretty cool, eh?

FIGURE 8.20   The player is prompted to automagically download and install the server's installed resource pack.

Whooee, adding Faithful sure does improve those Minecraft textures! Have a look for yourself in Figure 8.21.

FIGURE 8.21 The Faithful 32x32 resource pack doubles Minecraft's native display resolution. You can make an even crazier world by adding the Optifine mod to your server and clients.

Mapping Your Server to a Domain

As nice as MCProHosting's subdomain naming service is, you are still faced with the limitation of uniqueness. What do I mean?

You'll remember that MCProHosting uses mcph.co as their "root" DNS domain. When you choose a subdomain for your server, this needs to be a unique name across their entire customer base. This means that there's no way you'll get a common name like "play" or "minecraft" because another customer claimed those names a long time ago.

In my case, I own the DNS domain timwarnertech.com; it's where I host my business website. Wouldn't it be cool if I could map my Minecraft server's address to something like play.timwarnertech.com?

I'd like that.

Domain Name Mapping with GoDaddy

GoDaddy (http://godaddy.com) is my domain and web host, and MCProHosting actually has a dedicated Knowledgebase article on domain mapping with GoDaddy (http://bit.ly/1KaiU0O).

I'll begin by logging in to my GoDaddy account and opening the Domain Manager page for my timwarnertech.com domain.

All web hosts in my experience provide an interface that allows you to manage your domain's DNS records. Recall that DNS records map a user-friendly hostname to an IP address.

Speaking of IP address, we'll need to revisit our Minecraft server control panel and fetch our server's public IP address and port combination.

With MCProHosting, you go to your My Server page and copy the Server Address value, which in my case is as follows:

```
198.24.162.90:59248
```

We need to add two new records to my timwarnertech.com DNS zone:

Host (A) record: This one maps the name "server" to our Minecraft server's public IP address.

Service (SRV) record: This one maps the Minecraft network service to the server. timwarnertech.com host record.

You can pick up the suggested A and SRV record details in Figures 8.22 and 8.23.

FIGURE 8.22 Our custom host (A) record.

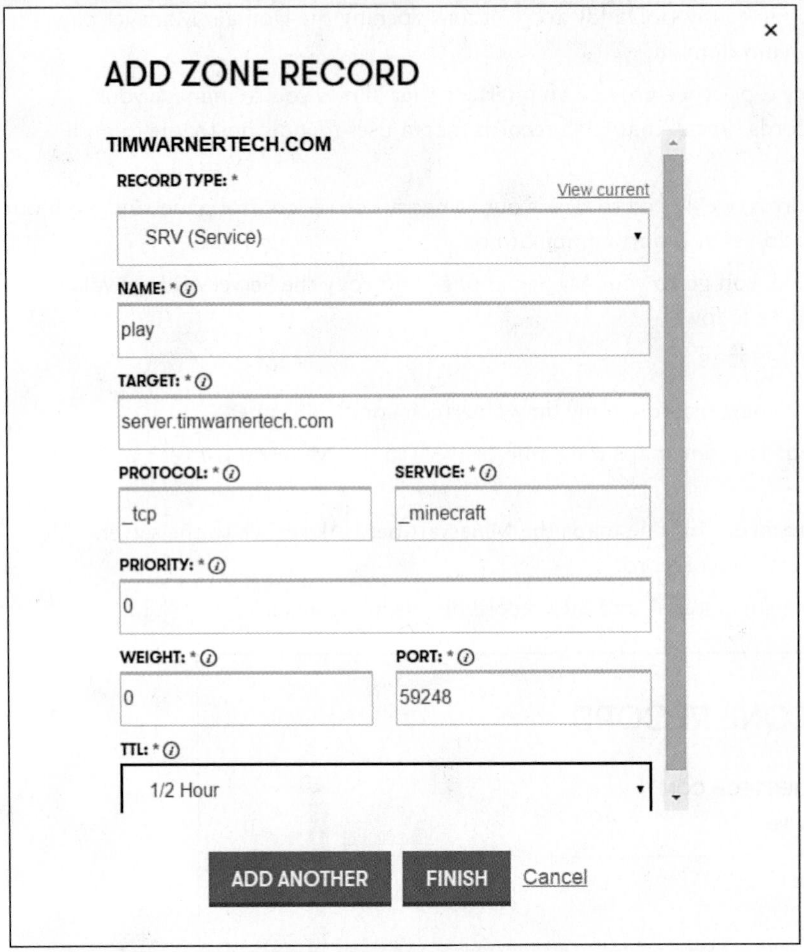

FIGURE 8.23 Our custom service (SRV) record.

To wrap up this discussion in a tidy little package, your users will use your custom domain name when they add your server to their Minecraft client applications (see Figure 8.24).

FIGURE 8.24 Connecting to our Minecraft server by using a custom DNS domain name. Notice the Server Resource Packs option; this is set to "Prompt" by default.

A Brief Roster of Other Well-Regarded Minecraft Hosting Companies

I'd be remiss if I didn't give some additional options for third-party Minecraft hosts that receive top ratings from the Minecraft community.

The following list is by no means comprehensive. Additionally, you need to know that I haven't personally tested all the hosts in this list; you need to practice your own due diligence before you commit your money, time, and effort to a host, even if only for one month.

Ownage Hosting: http://ownagehosting.com/

GGServers: https://ggservers.net/

BeastNode: https://www.beastnode.com/

Bisect Hosting: https://www.bisecthosting.com/

Creeper Host: http://www.creeperhost.net/

TIP

The Minecraft Forum is a current, comprehensive resource for information on Minecraft server hosting companies: http://www.minecraftforum.net/forums/servers/minecraft-server-hosting.

The Bottom Line

Third-party Minecraft hosts are awesome, and by now you understand the basic vocabulary used by these hosts. You know the things to look for (and to avoid) in the Minecraft hosting marketplace.

Regardless of whether you choose MCProHosting or another service, you truly become an honest-to-goodness Minecraft server operator after you have a publicly accessible server online.

In the next chapter we'll go through the generally agreed-on best practices for operating your online Minecraft server day to day. We'll address stuff like protecting your server from griefing and abuse, creating attractive and powerful world spawn points, and more. See you then!

> "The best way to find yourself is to lose yourself in the service of others."
>
> —Mahatma Gandhi

Giving Your Players the Best Gaming Experience

What You'll Learn in This Chapter:

- Protecting your server from abuse
- Customizing the world spawn
- Supporting multiple worlds
- Mastering the art of teleportation

Think for a moment about the best experiences you've had as a player on a Minecraft online server. What was the main thing that helped you to feel so comfortable? I would hazard a guess that "helpful admins" probably topped your list.

Minecraft servers that are run by people who genuinely care about their connected users (and their hard build work) are the successful ones. By contrast, Minecraft admins who host servers simply to make money, gather personal information from players, and the like have no long-term viability (fortunately) in the Minecraft multiplayer community.

We'll focus this chapter on some solid, practical ways that you can both protect your Minecraft server and give your players the kind of experience that they want to return to again and again and again. As usual, we have much material to cover, so let's get started.

Protecting Your Server from Abuse

"Abuse" in a Minecraft multiplayer context refers to players who connect to online Minecraft servers with the intent of interacting with the service in unauthorized ways. The motivation for Minecraft server abusers varies; however, we can outline some general purposes:

Anarchy: These people destroy players' builds, steal their property, and even kill their avatars simply because they want to cause as much mayhem as possible before their account is banned by an OP.

Identify Theft: As a player, you should *never* give out personally identifiable information on a Minecraft server because there are individuals who connect simply to mine identity data for nefarious purposes.

Hacktivism: Your PVC might not be targeted specifically, but sometimes gangs of online vigilantes attempt to take down an entire hosting provider in order to prove some ideological point.

Distributed Denial-of-Service Attack

A denial-of-service (DoS) attack occurs when a person abuses technology to overload a target system with bogus and/or malformed network messages. The overloaded machine is taken offline, which produces, well, a denial of service to connected users.

Distributed denial-of-service (DDoS) attacks are much larger-scale, coordinated attacks. You can see what a DDoS attack looks like from a bird's-eye perspective in Figure 9.1.

What's fascinating about DDoS attacks is that most of the "bots" in a DDoS "army" are residential home computers that were infected by DDoS agent software due to user mistakes such as opening unfamiliar email attachments or visiting the wrong website. In most cases, the end user never realizes that his or her computer is being used as a "slave" in a bot army.

However, in my experience your home-based server probably will never be the target of DDoS attacks simply because you're not a big enough target.

By contrast, as I said earlier, if you're renting a virtual private server (VPC) from a Minecraft hosting company, a DDoS attack against your provider will by definition affect your server's uptime as well.

The good news is that any Minecraft hosting company worth its salt includes DDoS protection/remediation technologies in their service level agreements (SLAs) with their customers.

For example, Intreppid (https://www.intreppid.com/) is a Minecraft hosting company that differentiates itself from its competition based on its DDoS protection offering.

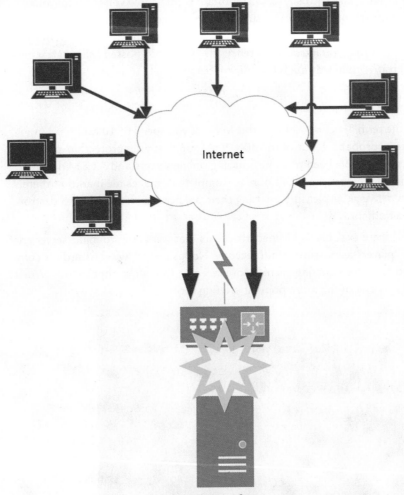

FIGURE 9.1 A DDoS attack can involve tens of thousands of attackers.

What to Do to Prevent DDoS Attacks

As I see it, you have two choices for minimizing the chance that your hosted Minecraft server will be taken offline due to a DDoS attack:

- Join a Minecraft hosting company that includes DDoS protection in its service plans.
- Pay for DDoS protection separately.

Companies such as CloudFlare (https://www.cloudflare.com/) allow you to route your Minecraft server's traffic through them as a subscription service. The benefit here is that CloudFlare intercepts all incoming traffic to your server and will protect it from DDoS attacks. The trade-off is that you introduce latency (delay) in your hosted Minecraft games because, again, all traffic routes through CloudFlare before it gets to your players.

Griefing

We've mentioned the term "griefing" a lot in this book. If you speak to 10 random Minecraft server operators, probably 8 out of the 10 will tell you that grief protection is one of their core duties as an OP. I've been to some amazing online servers and seen Minecraft builds that must have taken hundreds of hours to complete. It makes me mad that there exist "players" who derive great pleasure by using their pickaxes, lava, and TNT to destroy the precious work of others.

If you can believe it, there exist hacked Minecraft clients that were built to make server griefing as easy for the "player" as possible. Until recently, Nodus (http://www.wizardhax.com/nodus/) was the go-to hacked griefing client. More recently, though, it appears that Wurst, shown in Figure 9.2, is one of the more popular griefing tools.

FIGURE 9.2   As you can see, Wurst is a hacked client that makes big changes to the Minecraft client interface.

CAUTION

I won't provide instructions on how to find and install griefing clients in this book because there's too big of a chance that your computer will become infected with malware. It should come as no surprise that the pursuit of hacked Minecraft clients leads you into a thorny thicket of AdFly pages, drive-by downloads, and other opportunities for malware infection.

Hack Yourself

Even though I'm not providing you with instructions on finding and installing Wurst (you should be able to handle that yourself if you've studied this book thoroughly thus far), I nonetheless suggest that you consider launching periodic griefing attacks on your own server, both with and without griefing tools.

TIP

If you use the Google Chrome browser (which you certainly should be doing, in my humble opinion), then consider adding the AdF.ly Skipper extension (http://is.gd/pXCs7R) to protect you from that maddening flurry of pop-ups that AdF.ly normally unleashes on you when try to fetch a file download.

The benefits of this approach should be clear: By attempting to attack your own server, you can discover for yourself how vulnerable your server is. How else, for example, can you quickly and easily test that your Bukkit plugins are in fact blocking cracked Minecraft clients?

The Wurst tool in particular has a robust user interface that is accessible to the griefer in-game. You can see this menu in Figure 9.3.

FIGURE 9.3 Griefing tools such as Nodus and Wurst (pictured here) make it simple for a griefer to cause all sorts of in-game mischief on online Minecraft server worlds.

Blocking Griefers

In the preceding chapter we signed up for hosted Minecraft with MCProHosting. We'll continue to use our MCProHosting account in the current chapter as we address how to use plugins to protect our server.

One of the most popular and effective antigriefing/anticheat Bukkit plugins is NoCheatPlus (http://dev.bukkit.org/bukkit-plugins/nocheatplus/). According to the project page I gave you, NoCheatPlus includes logic to protect your Minecraft worlds from problems such as the following:

- Unauthorized flying and speed-moving
- Fighting hacks
- Fast block breaking
- Nukers that destroy large parts of the map
- Inventory hacks
- Chat spam

Griefing clients such as Wurst and Nodus exploit vulnerabilities in the Minecraft code, and sometimes plugin or mod code. Antigriefing plugins such as NoCheatPlus can't block connections from cracked Minecraft clients, but they can at least try to block the execution of those exploits.

To conduct our tests, I will start by installing NoCheatPlus on my hosted Minecraft server; then I'll use the Wurst hacked Minecraft client to log in to my world and try to cause trouble.

The bad news is that, depending on your Minecraft and Wurst versions, Wurst is able to mostly bypass NoCheatPlus protection. For example, I enabled the Jesus hack that allows my Steve to walk on water, as shown in Figure 9.4.

FIGURE 9.4 Sadly, some hacked Minecraft clients can work around antigriefing protection such as NoCheatPlus.

CAUTION

As an OP you'll need to watch your server log closely to trap false positives. You might have one or more users hung up on your server because your antigriefing tools identify that user as a hacker. Communication and close server monitoring are central to your success!

In my continued testing I found that I could use Nodus 2.0 and its "Nuker" hack to pulverize large parts of my shared world, as shown in Figure 9.5. Bummer!

FIGURE 9.5 Here I grief my own server by using the Nodus 2.0 hacked Minecraft client.

CoreProtect (http://www.curse.com/bukkit-plugins/minecraft/coreprotect) is another popular Minecraft antigriefing Bukkit plugin. The two capabilities that CoreProtect brings to your world are these:

- Fast rollback of damage caused by griefers
- Extensive, block-level logging so that you know exactly what's been done and by whom

The latter point is especially important. After all, identifying griefers is only half the battle. The next step is to use your "heavy hammer" console commands to deal with the threat. These commands, you'll remember, are as shown here:

/kick: Boots the griefer from your server.

/ban: Blocks the griefer's Minecraft username from your server.

/ban-ip: Blocks the griefer's IP address (this is useful if the griefer uses multiple Minecraft user accounts).

As an OP, you manage CoreProtect in-game by issuing console commands. For instance, typing /coreprotect or /co with no additional parameters displays the help, as shown in Figure 9.6.

I keep repeating how important it is to watch your Minecraft server log, but what does that actually look like in practice? Well, for starters, take a look at Figure 9.7, which shows my hosted Minecraft server log.

FIGURE 9.6 CoreProtect provides excellent block logging and rollback to foil those pesky griefers.

FIGURE 9.7 With practice you'll identify malicious players quickly and deal with them just as fast.

MCProHosting color-codes the log, making it easier to pick out the "good stuff." Here, though, the good stuff is actually bad stuff. Look for WARN messages to point you to trouble on your server. The log reads from the bottom (oldest messages) to the top (newest messages).

In Figure 9.7 you can see that TechTrainerTim was auto-kicked for floating and flying. If you're running a Survival server, you know that the user is doing something he isn't supposed to because he shouldn't be able to fly in any circumstance.

The line that follows is also suspect. As you can see, I kicked the player and am in the process of banning his account. Good riddance!

```
[Server] WARN TechTrainerTim moved too quickly!
```

Tips for Addressing Griefers

This griefing and antigriefing discussion got very dense very quickly. Let me summarize my best tips for you in bulleted list form:

- **Install antigriefing plugins on your server:** Do this but be mindful of versions. In general, later plugin and Minecraft versions fix vulnerabilities that were exposed in earlier versions.

- **Keep an eye on server logs:** Pay particular attention to warnings and errors.

- **If you don't need it, don't install it:** You might have vulnerabilities in plugins that you don't even use. When in doubt, uninstall.

- **Communicate with your players:** Remember that you might get false positives. Consider private-messaging players by using /tell and evaluating their replies to confirm their intentions on your server.

Customizing the World Spawn

The world spawn is important in Minecraft multiplayer because this is the initial starting point for all your incoming players. To that end, many Minecraft server administrators spend considerable time customizing the spawn "lobby," covering details such as these:

- Tutorials to help players understand your server rules

- Directions to minigame areas

- Entry points to additional worlds

One of my favorite family-friendly Minecraft servers is TownCraft (play.towncraft.us). Check out Figure 9.8 to see the server's massive spawn area.

NOTE

If you look into the distance in Figure 9.8, you'll see a collection of teleportation portals. These warp the player to other TownCraft worlds; we'll cover how to do this later in this chapter.

FIGURE 9.8   I enjoy TownCraft's (play.towncraft.us) world spawn. Big signs point you to Survival, Creative, and Minigame worlds.

Setting the Server Spawn

Assuming that you're logged in to the shared world as OP, walk Steve to where you want the server spawn point located and run the following console command:

```
/setworldspawn
```

To find the exact coordinates that correspond to your world's server spawn, download a tool such as NBTExplorer (http://bit.ly/1BWlrrs) and expand the `level.dat` node. As shown in Figure 9.9, the SpawnX, SpawnY, and SpawnZ coordinates are your world spawn.

We covered the `server.properties` file when we first learned how to set up Minecraft server. Let me remind you that the spawn-protection property denotes an area surrounding your world spawn that non-OPs cannot destroy or otherwise modify. Thus, by setting the value like so:

```
spawn-protection=32
```

we guarantee that blocks contained within a radius of 32 blocks from the origin point won't disappear due to malicious or accidental changes by regular players. That's a good thing, believe me. After all, if your world spawn disappears, where will players spawn when they enter your shared world?

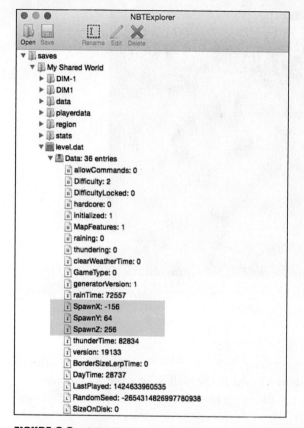

FIGURE 9.9 NBTExplorer allows us to peek into Minecraft's core configuration files; here we determine our world's spawn coordinates.

Building a Spawn Lobby

Yikes—this is a big subject. So big, in fact, that I'll draw your attention to my colleague James Floyd Kelly's excellent book *Engineering with Minecraft* for full details. The fastest way to create an impressive-yet-functional multiplayer spawn lobby is to make use of Minecraft .schematic files.

In a nutshell, a schematic is a prebuilt Minecraft asset. The Minecraft community is full of artists and structural designers who create builds and make them freely available for download. For instance, adding a schematic might give you any of the following within seconds, saving you hours and hours of work:

- Multiplayer spawn lobbies

- 2D/3D pixel art

- Buildings (homes, castles, temples, and so on)

- Transportation (boats, flying machines, submarines)

- Roller coasters
- Dungeons

Here are some popular schematic sites that you might want to investigate:

- Minecraft-Schematics: http://www.minecraft-schematics.net/
- Reddit MinecraftSchematics: https://www.reddit.com/r/minecraftschematics/
- Minecraft Schematics: http://www.minecraft-schematics.com/
- MCSchematics: http://www.mcschematics.com/
- Planet Minecraft Schematics: http://www.planetminecraft.com/resources/projects/any/?share=schematic

Preparing the Land for a Lobby Schematic

I would hazard a guess that your server's world is not of the ultraflat variety simply because that particular configuration is boring to most players (unless you're doing a minigame, of course).

The best practice is to use a terraforming tool to flatten part of your world's land to accommodate your schematics.

You can easily flatten selected portions of your world; there are two workflows that I use:

- MCEdit (http://www.mcedit.net/)
- WorldEdit (http://dev.bukkit.org/bukkit-plugins/worldedit/)

MCEdit is a separate tool that you run from outside of Minecraft. One important word of warning: Be sure to close the Minecraft client when you're doing world editing; having both programs running at the same time increases the risk that you'll damage your world.

MCEdit has a learning curve to it; I'll spend just a moment giving you the highest-level view (so to speak) of how to use it. Because WorldEdit is a simple Bukkit plugin and all configurations can be performed by an OP in-game, that's where I'll spend more time.

To get started, open MCEdit and browse to locate your target world's `level.dat` file. If your world is hosted on an online server, you'll need to download your world, edit the world on your local computer, and then upload/overwrite the server-based world.

You use both the keyboard and the mouse to navigate in MCEdit. Specifically, right-click to swivel the camera, use "WASD" to move around, and press Space and Shift to move up and down, respectively.

The trick to flattening land is that you want to left-click to place the selection box on a representative block that exists at the height you want your land flattened to. The Nudge controls allow you to expand your selection in three dimensions.

After you've used the keyboard and mouse to fill your selection, you use the Delete Blocks command from the left-hand navigation menu (shown in Figure 9.10).

FIGURE 9.10 MCEdit is a great Minecraft terraforming tool, but it requires local access to your world's `level.dat` file.

You commit your changes in MCEdit by pressing Ctrl+S. Close MCEdit and log in to your world. Your terraforming edits will appear! You can see the impressive sight in my shared world in Figure 9.11.

FIGURE 9.11 Now that I've flattened some land, I'm ready to load some schematics and make a dynamite spawn lobby for my server.

WorldEdit—A More Flexible Terraforming Solution

I use WorldEdit both for modeling Minecraft land and for importing schematics. This is why I prefer WorldEdit to MCEdit—the former is simply more flexible.

FOLLOW ME!

Flatten Land with WorldEdit

In this exercise, we'll use WorldEdit to flatten a small patch of land in our Minecraft world. Because WorldCraft is a plugin and is used in-game, you don't have to worry about downloading and uploading your world files to your host. I'm assuming that you've already followed the steps I provided earlier to install WorldEdit on your server. Let's begin!

1 Find a spot on your map that you want to level.

2 Invoke the "magic wand" (really a wooden shovel!):

```
//wand
```

Minecraft responds this way:

```
Left click: select pos #1; Right click: select pos #2
```

3 Using your shovel-wand, right-click the first block you want to level, and then right-click the second. Think of your selection area as a rectangle in which the first position is one corner and the second position is the opposite corner. To illustrate, look at Figure 9.12, in which I mark my first and second positions.

FIGURE 9.12 With WorldEdit, you use your "magic wand" to select your target area.

4 Now we can remove those blocks by issuing the `//set` command:

```
//set 0
```

5 You might need to repeat steps 2 to 4 a few more times until you've flattened all you want to flatten. My final result is shown in Figure 9.13.

FIGURE 9.13   My land is flattened and ready to receive some schematic goodness!

TIP

WorldEdit has far more terraforming commands than you've learned here. Please read a command reference for more information. Here's one such page to get you started: http://wiki.sk89q.com/wiki/WorldEdit/Reference.

Using WorldEdit to Drop in a Schematic

On your Bukkit server, whether hosted locally or in the cloud, go ahead and install the WorldEdit plugin from http://dev.bukkit.org/bukkit-plugins/worldedit/. Restart the server as usual.

Next, enter the `plugins\WorldEdit` folder and create a subfolder called `schematics`. This folder will, of course, hold any `.schematic` files you download.

Now visit some good Minecraft schematic sites and download any `.schematic` files that interest you. For the sake of this example, I'll use a Tavern schematic I downloaded.

I'd recommend that you rename the `.schematic` using a simple, short name. I renamed my Tavern schematic `tavern.schematic`, simply enough.

Now log in to your shared world, OP yourself, and locate the land area that you flattened earlier. To load my tavern schematic into memory, I'll type

```
//schematic load tavern
```

Minecraft will respond with

```
tavern loaded. Paste it with //paste
```

Notice that we're using a double forward slash instead of a single slash like we normally use. Let's do this!

```
//paste
```

The result of my tavern "instabuild" is shown in Figure 9.14.

FIGURE 9.14 Using schematics is addicting because you can add such awesome builds with little to no effort required.

> ## CAUTION
>
> Aside from my recommendation to flatten land before placing a schematic, be aware that loading large schematics can all too easily crash your server. If this happens, stop the server and restart. I've never had my world get corrupted, but you might need to boost the working memory given to your server in your startup script to accommodate the temporary resource spike.

Supporting Multiple Worlds and Teleportation

Imagine for a moment that you're hosting a Bukkit server and gaining serious traction with a Survival world. You have a dedicated player community, and all is well. However, lately you've received requests from several players who want you to deploy a Creative world. Other players are requesting a "Hunger Games" world, and so on. Is it possible to host multiple logical worlds on a single Minecraft server?

Of course, the answer is yes.

Using Multiverse

Start by downloading and installing the Multiverse Core (http://dev.bukkit.org/bukkit-plugins/multiverse-core/) and Multiverse Portals (http://dev.bukkit.org/bukkit-plugins/multiverse-portals/) plugins. Reboot the server as usual.

We use Multiverse Core to deploy multiple worlds on our Bukkit server. We use Multiverse Portals to create teleportation portals to move players in between worlds. Take a look at Figure 9.15 to see what I'm planning on my Spigot server.

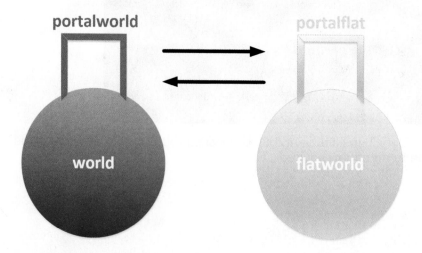

FIGURE 9.15 Schematic diagram of my server's two-world Multiverse setup.

As you can see in Figure 9.15, I create two portals to link my default world (named, by default, "world") and my second, created world, named "flatworld," that uses the superflat template.

Creating and Teleporting Between Worlds

Join your multiplayer world as an OP and use the following command to create a new superflat world named "flatworld":

```
/mv create flatworld normal -t flat
```

Minecraft responds with this:

```
Starting creation of world 'flatworld'...
Complete!
```

You can leave off the -t flat part if you want a traditional biome mix. Instead of normal you can substitute nether or end if you want to create those kinds of worlds.

Now let's list our worlds; Multiverse shows the default Minecraft world in addition to any that you create:

```
/mv list
```

Here's what Minecraft responded with on my Spigot v1.7.9 server:

```
====[ Multiverse World List ]====
Page 1 of 1
flatworld - NORMAL
world_the_end - THE_END
world_nether - NETHER
world - NORMAL
```

By the way, if we wanted to delete flatworld, we'd issue the following command:

```
/mvp remote flatworld
```

Let's teleport ourselves to the flatworld now:

```
/mv tp flatworld
```

Cool, eh? Now let's return to the original, default world:

```
/mv tp world
```

Deploying Portals

One thing that's awesome about Multiverse Portals is that your portals can be any size, any shape, and created from any material in the game. I'm serious! No messing around with obsidian and the ol' flint and steel.

To that point, go ahead and build yourself a portal frame. You can see my "snow frame" in Figure 9.16.

FIGURE 9.16 Although your portals can be made of any material, you might want to use the traditional materials so that your players instantly recognize the structures as such.

Remember how we used the WorldEdit wand to select land? You can actually use this wand to define your portal boundaries (the command is //wand), but Multiverse Portals actually has its own wand:

```
/mvp wand
```

CAUTION

I've had problems in the past creating portals when I had both WorldEdit and Multiverse Portals installed on the same server. You can fix this by temporarily disabling WorldEdit and using the Portals wand to create your portals.

As we did earlier, left-click to select one corner of the portal frame and then right-click the opposite corner. We're now ready to create our portalworld portal:

```
/mvp create portalworld
```

After you create your portal, give yourself a bucket of water and then place some water inside the portal frame. You can see how cool this looks in Figure 9.17.

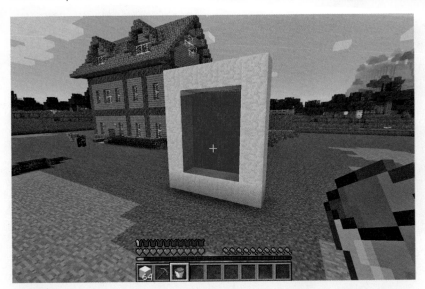

FIGURE 9.17   You can give your Multiverse portals a traditional feel by placing water inside the portal frame.

Teleport to the flatworld, give yourself a wand, mark your coordinates, and build a second portal frame named portalflat:

```
/mv tp flatworld
/mvp wand
/mvp create portalflat
```

We can run the /mvp list command to retrieve a list of all known portals:

```
--- Portals ---
portalflat   portalworld
```

You can see my flatworld portal in Figure 9.18.

FIGURE 9.18 I opted for traditional obsidian for my flatworld portal.

Connecting the Two Worlds

Our final step is to link the two portals so that users can teleport from one to the other. It's true that you can set a portal's destination during portal creation (read the Multiverse Portals documentation at https://github.com/Multiverse/Multiverse-Portals/wiki for details). However, I thought it "cleaner" to separate portal creation and management.

If you're following along, your Steve is standing in front of portalflat. Let's formally select the portal in the game:

```
/mvp select
```

Now we'll set portalflat's destination to portalworld:

```
/mvp modify dest p:portalworld
```

Minecraft then responds with this:

```
Property dest of Portal portalflat was set to p:portalworld
```

Walk through your new portal—you should find yourself in the default world almost instantly! We're almost finished. We need to connect portalworld to portalflat:

```
/mvp select portalworld
/mvp modify dest p:portalflat
```

NOTE

By default, only OPs can use Multiverse portals. To give ordinary players permission, configure PermissionsEx to grant the permission *multiverse.portal.access.PORTALNAME* (where *PORTALNAME* is the name of one of your portals) to those users.

Any additional worlds that you create in Multiverse are every bit as "real" as the default worlds. For proof, open your server's folder and see for yourself. If you're not near your server, examine my Spigot server in Figure 9.19.

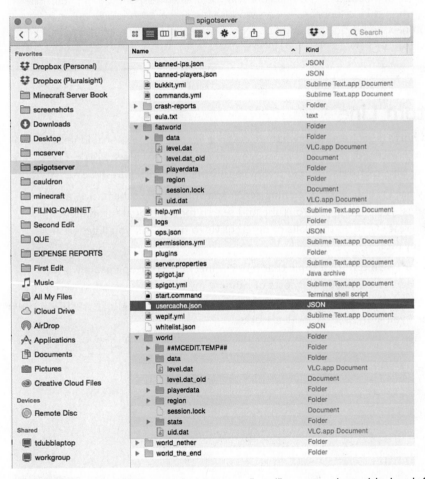

FIGURE 9.19   Multiverse worlds are as "real" as any that ship by default in the game.

NOTE

BungeeCord (http://www.spigotmc.org/wiki/bungeecord-faq/) is a standalone application that acts as a proxy on behalf of multiple Minecraft servers. In this chapter, we're hosting two worlds on one server. Imagine the power we could have by actually running different contexts (survival, creative, minigame, and so on) on totally separate server instances!

A "proxy" is a server or service that stands in place of one or more additional servers. So when you use BungeeCord, you advertise your Minecraft server under a single IP address, as usual, but the difference is players actually shuttle between different servers when they teleport between worlds. It's a cool technology, but is in my opinion too complex and expensive in all but the most popular online Minecraft servers.

The Bottom Line

Does your head hurt? If you're new to what we covered in this chapter, I would imagine that you feel pretty overwhelmed. If so, my best suggestion for you is to take a break. Take a day off from anything Minecraft-related, and return to this material with a fresh head.

To supplement what I taught you concerning server spawns, placing schematics, and hosting multiple worlds, you should visit YouTube and search for additional tutorials. Admittedly, you'll find great variety in the skills of different video hosts, but you'll get fresh perspectives at any rate.

In our final chapter, we'll turn to a topic that many Minecraft server operators wonder about, namely, "How can I recoup the costs of running my hosted Minecraft server?" The answer to that question is "monetization," and by the end of Chapter 10, "Monetizing Your Minecraft Server," you'll understand how it works.

"Making money is a hobby that will complement any other hobbies that you have, beautifully."

–Scott Alexander, author

Monetizing Your Minecraft Server

What You'll Learn in This Chapter:

- Understanding Minecraft server monetization
- Maintaining EULA compliance
- Setting up BuyCraft
- Advertising your Minecraft server

My five-year-old daughter, Zoey, absolutely loves Stampy Cat. Have you heard of him? The last time I checked, his stampylonghead YouTube channel (https://www.youtube.com/user/stampylonghead) had 5.6 million subscribers. That's a *lot* of eyeballs watching his Minecraft "Let's Play" videos.

Minecraft YouTubers such as Stampy make a great deal of money strictly through Google ads that play every time a viewer watches one of their videos. As Minecraft server operators, you might be interested in how to gain a loyal player following and perhaps even enjoy some monetary reward.

Through perseverance, hard work, and word of mouth, you might have a thriving server with lots of players. Many of these players might beg you to upgrade your server's RAM, add minigames, add more mods, and so forth. How can you pay for these additions? Monetization is an answer.

In this chapter we will focus on Minecraft monetization (the fancy term for "making money by doing something related to Minecraft"), but not so much with YouTube "Let's Play" vids.

Instead, I want to address the hows and whys of building a following and recouping any monetary costs that you incur by hosting a Minecraft server. Let's begin!

Understanding Mojang's Position on Minecraft Server Monetization

Until June 2014, Minecraft server operators had all sorts of ways not only to pay their hosting costs, but also to generate some honest-to-goodness profit:

- Charging players for item upgrades, kits, and so on
- Charging players for XP
- Creating an in-game money system that could be exchanged for real currency

Mojang, the original Minecraft developers, changed the Minecraft server community permanently when they published the landmark blog post "Let's Talk Server Monetisation!" on June 12, 2014 (https://mojang.com/2014/06/lets-talk-server-monetisation/). That article's June 16, 2014, follow-up, "Let's Talk Server Monetisation—The Follow-up Q+A" (https://mojang.com/2014/06/lets-talk-server-monetisation-the-follow-up-qa/), created an uproar among Minecraft server operators.

NOTE

The spelling "monetisation" instead of "monetization" reflects the European English spelling as opposed to the American spelling of this word. No typos in this book, I hope!

The New Minecraft EULA

The end user license agreement (EULA) represents what you are and are not allowed to do with Minecraft software. You see, one mistake many players make is believing that paying Mojang for a Minecraft single-user license gives them some kind of ownership of the game. Not true.

A software license grants you the rights to use the game, but again, only within the confines of the EULA.

I encourage you to read both of the aforementioned Mojang blog posts in their entirety. You should read the actual EULA (https://account.mojang.com/documents/minecraft_eula) as well.

In the meantime, let me snip out the most important EULA bullet points as they affect our lives as Minecraft server administrators:

- **You're allowed to charge players to access your server.** The notion here is that you're paying for your Minecraft hosting, so it's within your right to charge people for connection rights.

- **You're allowed to accept donations.** I'll show you how you can do this later in the chapter.

- **You're allowed to do in-game advertising.** Again, you'll understand how to implement this on your servers in a while.

- **You're not allowed to charge real-world currency for in-game money.** By doing this, Mojang thinks you're profiting from Mojang's proprietary game code, and they don't like that.

- **You're not allowed to pretend to be Mojang.** This is a nuanced point, but Mojang wants you to be clear in how you advertise your server that you are in no way affiliated with or endorsed by Mojang.

NOTE

I've spoken almost exclusively of Mojang throughout this book. I'm sure you know that Microsoft purchased Mojang for US$2.5 billion in September 2014. As of this writing in spring 2015, Microsoft has been silent on how it will direct Minecraft going forward. For that reason, and the fact that Mojang branding appears in the game, I've chosen to reference Mojang. To be sure, I'm as interested in you are to see how and when Microsoft begins to affect the Minecraft empire now that they own the source code.

The Backlash Against Mojang

By reading the new Minecraft EULA, you can easily see why these changes angered many Minecraft server operators. It's human nature to get upset if another entity does something that threatens your income stream.

As I write this chapter, I see that the Change.org petition "Change Your EULA!" (https://www.change.org/p/mojang-change-your-eula) has 23.5 thousand supporters. Wow.

Now what happens if you run a Minecraft server in violation of the Minecraft EULA—will the police come arrest you? Will you get a call from Mojang? Well, it is feasible, especially going forward with Microsoft owning Minecraft, that you might indeed receive a "takedown" notice if your server appears on Mojang/Microsoft's radar and is offering services that conflict with their EULA.

You already know that Minecraft servers operate by default in "online mode," which means that all incoming connection requests are verified as legal accounts in the Mojang user account database.

Monetizing Minecraft While Maintaining EULA Compliance

We'll assume as a matter of course that we plan to follow the Minecraft EULA as we prepare our server(s) for public connections. This means we need to answer the following question:

How can we finance our server costs and not run into legal compliance problems with Mojang?

I'll outline four possibilities for you:

- Donations
- In-game advertisements and sponsorship
- Cosmetic upgrade sales
- VIP server access

Donations

Mojang says that we server operators can both charge for game access and accept voluntary donations from our players. However, and this is crucial, we are not allowed to sell any game assets to our players that give them an advantage.

In other words, Mojang forbids server OPs from running "pay to win" scenarios. This makes sense from a gamesmanship standpoint. If player A spends real money to purchase XP and an enchanted diamond sword from your server, then that player has an advantage over nonspending players.

So yeah—how do we go about asking our players for money without getting spammy and/or obnoxious? First of all, we aren't allowed to reward donators with Minecraft gameplay features—that violates the EULA.

One novel approach is gifting the entire server player population with XP and/or game assets when any player donates. This transaction benefits all players, gives the donator an ego boost, and potentially encourages other players to make a donation in the name of altruism.

So how do you set this up?

BuyCraft (http://www.BuyCraft.net) is a donation/webstore Bukkit plugin that is, in a word, amazing. We'll cover how to set up BuyCraft later in the chapter; I'd prefer to stick to practical examples for now.

Let's say that we created a BuyCraft package that gives the selected player a diamond pickaxe for a US$1 donation. Yes, I know that to be EULA-compliant, we need to code the package for all online players. Sadly, doing that requires some research and a bit of coding/hacking because BuyCraft was originally designed before the 2014 EULA dustup.

From in-game, we need to periodically broadcast an announcement to remind players they can donate to our server in exchange for an item package. Plenty of Minecraft announcement plugins exist; in this example I'm using Announcement (http://dev.bukkit.org/bukkit-plugins/announcement/) because it's so easy to use.

Download the Announcement `.jar`, put it in your server's `plugins` folder, and reboot the server. Log in to your world as an OP and run the following command to show the plugin syntax:

```
/announce help
```

You can see the help output in Figure 10.1. In the meantime, read the Announcement Bukkit page to get detailed syntax help and examples.

FIGURE 10.1 The Announcement plugin works like most other Bukkit plugins.

TIP

It's an art and a science to strike a balance between keeping your players informed of your offerings and spamming them with constant messages. If players get annoyed and/or distracted by your announcements, they'll disconnect and likely won't return.

Let's create a simple announcement and set its repeat interval at 10 minutes. We first need to get a list of active announcements:

```
/announce list
```

You should see that ID 1 is a demo announcement. Let's get rid of that:

```
/announcement remove 1
```

Now we'll add a new message to the announcement list and set the interval:

```
/announce add Type /buy to make a donation. Diamond pickaxes only
$1! :)
/announce interval 600
```

You can see the announcement message in Figure 10.2.

FIGURE 10.2 Server announcements are an effective way to encourage donations, but be careful about not overdoing them.

From the buyer's perspective, all they have to do is type /buy at the Minecraft client command line; the result is shown in Figure 10.3.

As you can see in Figures 10.4 and 10.5, BuyCraft first prompts players to click a link to visit your BuyCraft webstore (they'll be asked to confirm that choice), and then complete the purchase by using an authorized payment method. Easy as pie! As an OP, your chosen payment gateway will reflect an incoming credit.

FIGURE 10.3   When the player types /buy, the player sees a matrix of all your published BuyCraft packages. To make a purchase, the player moves an item to a bottom inventory slot.

FIGURE 10.4   The user is directed from the Minecraft client to your BuyCraft webstore.

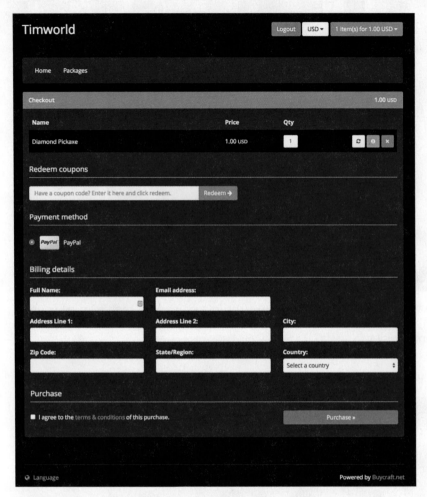

FIGURE 10.5 This payment screen should look familiar to almost anyone who has participated in an online purchase.

What's ingenious about BuyCraft is that the packages you create in your webstore simply send your server a console command of your choosing after the payment is received.

In-Game Advertising and Sponsorship

Now let's get into how to use the Adventurize (http://www.adventurize.com/) Bukkit plugin to automate in-game advertising. The plugin generates periodic ads inside your shared server world, and you get paid every time a player clicks an ad link.

NOTE

You might want to check out AdCraft (http://adcraft.io/), another in-game advertising Bukkit plugin.

To get started, visit adventurize.com and create a free account. Download the plugin, place the .jar in the server's plugins folder, and restart.

From the Adventurize web portal, you'll add your Minecraft server's public IP address and obtain your account authentication token. Paste the authentication token value in the plugin's config.yml, reboot the server again, and you're all set.

As of this writing, Adventurize is in beta (testing) mode and, according to their website, won't run ads in your Minecraft world until they launch. To get a feel for what in-game advertising looks like, though, you can see a representative screenshot from an AdCraft-enabled server in Figure 10.6.

FIGURE 10.6   This is an AdCraft-generated ad running in a Minecraft multiplayer world. (Image credit: adcraft.io)

Cosmetic Upgrade Sales

This Mojang EULA situation does put some crimps on what we can do as Minecraft server operators. We are free to sell "cosmetic" upgrades—in other words, Minecraft assets and features that don't affect core gameplay and give a player an advantage over other players.

Curiously, Mojang forbids us from gifting or selling capes (they give custom cape skins to players whom they identify as valuable community members).

So what are some examples of "cosmetic" stuff that we can sell to our players? Well, maybe the following, in part:

- Pet (animal mobs along with taming foods, like a sheep with a bundle of wheat)
- Hat or noncape, non-armor skin component
- Custom name/title/prefix

As a case study, I created a free BuyCraft package that gives the player a wolf and a bone with which to tame it. Again, we'll learn how to set up BuyCraft momentarily. After the player types /buy and selects the Free Wolf package, the player is taken to the BuyCraft website to complete the "purchase." Notice in Figure 10.7 that the player goes through the same payment gateway even for free packages.

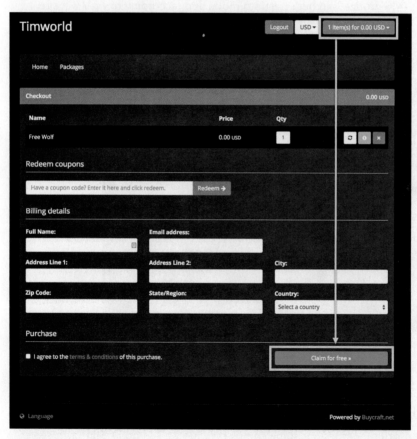

FIGURE 10.7   The player doesn't have to be intimidated by the BuyCraft "buy" page; note that this package is free and requires no payment method.

TIP

As a server operator, you can use free packages as a way to test your packages' functionality. I spend quite a bit of time debugging my packages before I'm comfortable releasing them for purchase or redemption by my players.

To conduct the test, simply type /buy and redeem a free package just like your players do.

Within a few minutes the player will receive notification that the transaction is complete. Look at Figure 10.8; this happy player now has a wolf to tame.

FIGURE 10.8 Giving your players free packages not only is EULA-friendly but also makes your players feel more a part of your Minecraft server community.

VIP Server Access or Subscriptions

Very Important Person (VIP) server access appeals to the human need to feel unique, special, and different. You can combine BuyCraft with the VIP Bukkit plugin (http://dev.bukkit.org/bukkit-plugins/vip/) to give players priority access to your server.

For example, let's suppose that your Minecraft server has 25 player slots. A player decides that she wants a VIP account, issues /buy in the Minecraft client console, selects the VIP membership option, pays for the order, and receives the VIP designation.

What this means in practice is that this VIP player will always be able to log in to your server. Under the hood, the VIP plugin (a) detects an incoming connection request from a VIP, and (b) kicks the most recent non-VIP player and attaches the VIP player to the open slot. Specifically, you'd create a BuyCraft package that issues the `/vip add Player` command after a purchase. As you'll learn shortly, you can add multiple server commands to a package, so in this case you'd include a server subscription along with the VIP status. That is, unless you want your paid VIPs to retain their status forever.

The BuyCraft website has an article on how to set up recurring subscriptions (https://www.BuyCraft.net/community/article/21/how-to-setup-recurring-subscriptions), but here is the basic workflow:

1 Connect to a subscription-friendly payment gateway (PayPal is on the list).

2 From your BuyCraft account page, configure the payment gateway to accept subscriptions.

3 Change the package type to "Subscription."

4 Profit!

Setting Up BuyCraft

Before we can design and sell/give packages to our players, we need to create our BuyCraft account and create a payment gateway.

FOLLOW ME!

Creating a BuyCraft Account

In this exercise, we'll create a free BuyCraft account. If you plan to use BuyCraft heavily, you might want to consider purchasing a paid account (https://www.buycraft.net/pricing). The premium account levels give you much more flexibility in terms of payment gateways, connected Minecraft servers, maximum number of packages, and so on.

1 Point your web browser to buycraft.net and click the Sign Up link. The registration is pretty uneventful: You'll specify your e-mail address along with a password, and you'll be asked to confirm your e-mail address.

2 The real fun starts in the BuyCraft setup wizard (see Figure 10.9). Your first choice is to choose an easy-to-remember name for your webstore. Remember that this address is shown to your users in-game, so make it obvious that your players aren't getting redirected to some gnarly spam or phishing site.

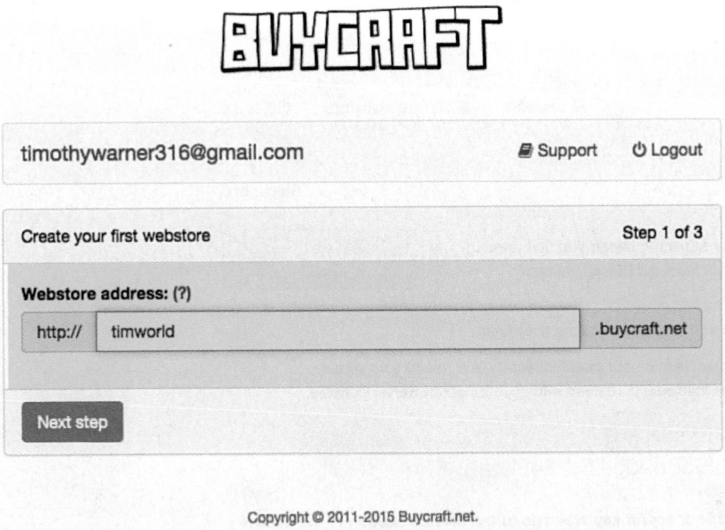

FIGURE 10.9   You might want to name your BuyCraft webstore after your Minecraft server name for consistency.

3 As shown in Figure 10.10, click the Download link to be redirected to the Bukkit web-site. Download the plugin, pop it into your server's `plugins` folder, and restart the server. You have a lot of experience with doing that by now, that's for sure.

4 In the same web page you'll be given your secret key, a honking long alphanumeric string that ties your Minecraft server to your BuyCraft Webstore. You can see mine in Figure 10.10.

Copy the `/buycraft` secret lines to memory by selecting the data and pressing Ctrl+C (Windows) or Cmd+C (OS X). You'll then paste that command into your Minecraft server console. Make sure to remove the slash (/) from the command string, because you can use the slash only in-game and not in the server console. Minecraft will confirm that it accepted the key.

Timworld   🗏 Support   👤 Change webstore   ⏻ Logout

Plugin installation   Step 2 of 3

To install Buycraft on your Minecraft server you first need to download the Bukkit plugin from our BukkitDev page:

[📄 Download]

Follow the instructions below after downloading the plugin:

1. Place the Buycraft.jar file into your plugin directory and reload your server.
2. Copy and paste the following command into your Minecraft Server console:

/buycraft secret
796ced1b84d557d9d541b724f4

If you need to find your secret key again go to the servers section of the control panel.

3. Type the command **/buycraft**, if no errors are displayed you have successfully setup Buycraft!

[Next step]

Copyright © 2011-2015 Buycraft.net.

FIGURE 10.10 BuyCraft uses a Bukkit plugin `.jar` just like all the other plugins we've used in the course. The secret key is what ties your Minecraft server to your BuyCraft webstore.

5 After you confirm that you're using an online (legal) Minecraft server, you're taken to your BuyCraft dashboard. Click the Webstore link on the top navigation bar and then shift focus to the Gateways page.

A gateway is a merchant server that you'll use to receive and send money. In Figure 10.11 I give you a "mashup" screenshot that shows you the Gateways portal page and the (partial) list of supported gateways.

FIGURE 10.11 I've had no problems at all using PayPal as my BuyCraft payment gateway.

6 Now navigate to the Content page and click Packages. It's time to create a couple of packages!

Creating a Paid Package

On the Content, Packages page in your BuyCraft account portal, click Add Package to build a new package. For this first one we'll sell a diamond pickaxe for $1.

In Figure 10.12 you can see the configuration behind my Diamond Pickaxe package.

FIGURE 10.12 The underlying mechanism behind a package is pretty simple. The player sends a payment, and BuyCraft executes one or more Minecraft server commands to deploy the package contents.

We don't have the white space to do an in-depth how-to on BuyCraft. For that kind of detail, please spend time at the BuyCraft Community page (https://www.buycraft.net/community). Here are some quick notes that describe my choices shown in Figure 10.12:

- I uploaded a diamond pickaxe image to personalize the in-game package icon. This is a nice touch, and you should consider adding images. If you're looking for the best possible icons and are willing to pay for them, check out the Starter Icon Pack from CraftillDawn.com (http://craftilldawn.com/shop/starter-icon-pack/).

- I set my Expire After property to 0 months. This means that players can keep the pickaxe forever.

- I set the price to 1.00 USD. For free packages, type a 0.00 price.

In addition, pay close attention to the Commands portion in Figure 10.12. Adding useful metadata and a reasonable item price is one thing, but if you code your commands incorrectly, you'll wind up with unhappy, unsatisfied players if they don't get what they paid for in-game.

You remember how to use /give, correct? We use (almost) the same syntax in BuyCraft, with two exceptions:

- Leave off the slash (/) just as you would if you issued this command in the Minecraft server console

- Type {name} as a variable to represent the purchaser.

Thus, the following command completes the package configuration:

```
give {name} diamond_pickaxe 1
```

Giving a Paid Item to All Players

I'm sorry to harp on the Mojang EULA issue so often, but it truly is a big deal. Install and activate the GiveAllItems Bukkit plugin (http://dev.bukkit.org/bukkit-plugins/giveallitems/).

In your BuyCraft portal, go back to the Packages page and click the pencil icon to edit its contents. Let's change the command string to give the diamond shovel (spade) to all players whenever a person buys one:

```
/giveall 277 1
```

Observe in the preceding code that we specify the Minecraft item ID instead of a friendly object name. My favorite place to look up item IDs is the Minecraft ID List (http://minecraft-ids.grahamedgecombe.com/).

Anyway, you can see in Figure 10.13 that Zoey just received the spade even though it was another player who actually bought it. Cool! The EULA is happy!

zoey2010 joined the game.
Welcome, zoey2010!
Type /help for a list of commands.
Type /list to see who else is online.
Players online: 2 - World time: 6:00 AM
You have no new mail.
Welcome zoey2010 to the server!
Cleared all inventory items from zoey2010.
[GiveAllItems] You've just been given 1 diamond_spade from Te
chTrainerTim.

FIGURE 10.13 By combining BuyCraft with GiveAllItems, you can both accept donations and stay in compliance with the Mojang EULA.

Creating a Free Package

For our second sample package, let's say that we want to create a "garden pack" that gives two items in the same package:

- 16 Dandelion

- 16 Poppy

This is a similar type of package as in the Free Wolf example we used earlier in the chapter. I was thinking of making a "garden pack" that was more useful and contained the following items:

- Stone shovel

- Stone hoe

- 12 grass blocks

- Water bucket

However, one could make the argument that a player who bought (or was given, free) this garden pack would have an unfair advantage in the game. These are decisions you'll have to make for yourself.

In any event, check out Figure 10.14, which shows you how I built the free Garden Pack.

FIGURE 10.14 This free Garden Pack adds cosmetic value to the player's game. After all, who doesn't like to decorate their in-game yard?

As an OP, you'll need to issue /buycraft reload to refresh the in-game BuyCraft package environment.

All that players have to do is type /buy, select the Garden Pack, go to your webstore, and redeem the free package. Success!

Advertising Your Minecraft Server

The first guideline in advertising your server to the Minecraft community is to ensure that the server is "done." By that I mean you've taken care of all the major details:

- Nice spawn lobby with lots of player help (tutorial signs and so on)
- All plugins loaded, configured, and functional
- Interesting things to do in your world
- Permissions all sorted out

If players see your server advertised somewhere, show up, and observe an unfinished world, then they will quickly lose interest and leave. Worse, they might conclude that the OP is "asleep at the switch" and try griefing other players or hacking your server directly. Not good.

Where to Advertise

My Minecraft host, MCProHosting, provides a handy-dandy list of popular Minecraft server lists where you can advertise your server (reference: http://bit.ly/1EYOuKk):

http://minestatus.net

http://minecraftservers.org

http://minecraftservers.net

http://minecraftserverlist.eu

http://vote4craft.net/service

http://planetminecraft.com

http://minecraft-mp.com

http://topg.org

http://mineservers.com

http://minecraftserverland.com

https://mcserverstatus.com/servers

http://mcs-list.org

http://minetrack.net

http://minepick.com

http://mc-serverlist.com

https://minecraftiplist.com

http://minecraftserverfinder.com

http://minequery.net

http://gametracker.com

http://minecraftforum.net/

TIP

I included Planet Minecraft in the preceding list because you'll see the site referenced as a good place to register your server. Nevertheless, many of my Minecraft server operator friends told me they avoid that particular site because it tends to be a haven for griefers. These sad individuals join servers with the sole intention of wreaking as much havoc as possible. Be careful out there!

The Importance of the Server Status Banner

A Minecraft server status banner is a 468×60 animated GIF image that serves four purposes:

- To capture the attention of potential players
- To display your server's connection address
- To show the server's current status (online or offline)
- To list the number of currently connected players, and the total number of player slots

The good news is that you don't have to be a graphic artist like my wife, Susan, in order to build an effective status banner. Head over to TopG (http://topg.org/minecraft_banner_maker) and fill out the Banner Maker fields, as shown in Figure 10.15. You can't see the animation in a static image, of course, but TopG includes animation and gives you a nice banner image—free! The finished product is shown in Figure 10.16.

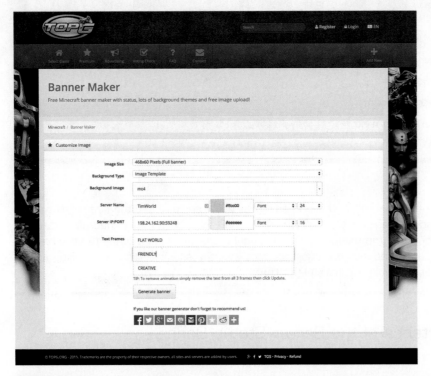

FIGURE 10.15 Minecraft server status banner generators are almost always free; TopG.org has a particularly nice design interface.

FIGURE 10.16 Here is my TopG Minecraft server status banner. Notice that the banner includes online status and number of online players.

Most Minecraft hosting companies give you a personalized server status banner; in Figure 10.17 you can see my MCProHosting server banner image.

FIGURE 10.17 My MCProHosting banner

You need to save not the source image but the URL to the image for use on Minecraft listing sites. For instance, here is my TopG embed code:

```
<a href="http://topg.org/Minecraft">
<img src="http://topg.org/image/100315/30638.gif"
alt="Best Minecraft Servers"></a>
```

NOTE

For Minecraft server banners to fetch online status, you'll need to set `enable-query=true` in your `server.properties` file.

Registering Your Minecraft Server

I strongly suggest that you record the following information in a text document before you start visiting Minecraft server lists to register your server; it will save you time and headaches, believe me:

- Your server IP address and port number
- The plugins you run
- The server features and game types that you offer
- The embed code for your banner image
- A short paragraph summing up your server's gaming philosophy

The actual registration process is uninteresting. You'll simply (a) create a free account on the site; and (b) use the site's Add Server form to include your Minecraft server in their lists.

Another good tip is to spend time studying the registration entries for the most popular Minecraft sites. A sample "mashup" is presented in Figure 10.18. Take note of the banner style, description, plugins, and so forth that contribute to those servers being so popular. Seek to emulate these successful servers as much as possible without outright ripping off their style.

Here are some trends I've seen in the registration entries for the world's most popular Minecraft servers:

- Server IP address uses a DNS hostname instead of a "raw" IP address and port
- Full branding (custom icon, banner image, font, logo, and so on)
- References to "friendly staff," diversity of gameplay
- Supports recent Minecraft version
- Has a YouTube channel and dedicated website

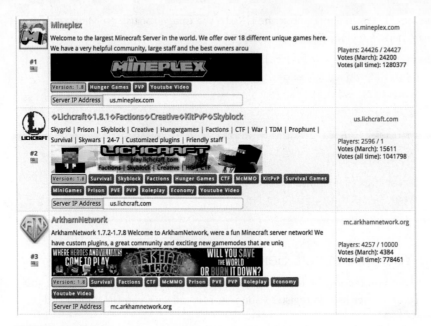

FIGURE 10.18 Spend time studying the registration entries for the most popular Minecraft servers at minecraft-server-list.com; you can learn a lot!

About Voting

In today's world of social media, most Minecraft players intuitively understand how to vote up their favorite Facebook posts, YouTube videos, and so forth. The Votifier Bukkit plugin (http://dev.bukkit.org/bukkit-plugins/votifier/) creates a lightweight "listener" on your Minecraft server that retrieves voting data from all Minecraft server lists that support it (which is the majority of them in my experience).

The more votes your server receives by players, the higher in the rankings your server appears. This is important because you need to actually show up in players' searches in order to show up on their connection radar.

Figure 10.19 shows you the voting mechanism on the Minecraft Server List (http://minecraft-server-list.com) registry.

FIGURE 10.19 The number of player votes your Minecraft server receives not only indicates your server's relative popularity, but also makes your server more visible in server lists.

Someplace to Compare Yourself

My five-year-old daughter, Zoey, and I are Minecraft partners; we play together nearly every night. Therefore, it should come as no surprise that I host only "family-friendly" Minecraft servers that kick/ban players who say or do non-family-friendly things. As a reference site for you to study, visit Cubeville (http://cubeville.org).

Even if you don't care about family-friendliness, Cubeville is a great source of what to do on your own server to maximize its potential for popularity. A representative in-game screenshot is shown in Figure 10.20.

New Cubeville players are required to work through an extensive tutorial before they're allowed into the world proper. I've found not only the staff but also the player population to be helpful and friendly. Cubeville has an in-game economy system with which you can earn "money" to spend on buildings, land, and so forth.

FIGURE 10.20 You could do worse than to emulate how Cubeville.org sets up their Minecraft server. Those folks really know what they're doing!

One final point concerning advertising your server: Make a custom server icon and format your message of the day (MOTD) text so that your server stands out in the Minecraft client. To see what I'm talking about, look at Cubeville's entry in Figure 10.21.

FIGURE 10.21 An often-overlooked branding element is the server icon and message of the day (MOTD).

Creating a Custom Server Entry for the Minecraft Client

Here's my "quick and dirty" recipe for adding a custom server icon to your Minecraft server:

1. Create or otherwise obtain a 64-pixel-by-64-pixel `.png` image file. You can convert pictures into an appropriately sized icon at sites like http://genfavicon.com. If you aren't an artist, download a premade 64×64 Minecraft-themed icon image from http://www.iconarchive.com/tag/minecraft-64x64 or another site like it.

2. Name the file `server-icon.png`. Be sure to use lowercase, and Minecraft needs the file to have that specific name.

3. Transfer `server-icon.png` to the root folder of your Minecraft server.

Customizing the MOTD

Again, let me provide you with a fast recipe for customizing and formatting your MOTD "blurb":

1 Open your `server.properties` file and find the `motd` property.

2 Add Minecraft formatting codes before the MOTD text you want to customize. Get the codes from The Minecraft Forum (http://bit.ly/1E3QK17) or another site you like. In this example, I format my MOTD to yellow:

```
\u00A7eTim's awesome Minecraft Server\!
```

Perform some additional research to learn how to animate the text. Be careful, though, because the line between a noticeable MOTD and a garish one is thin indeed. You can see my final customized server MOTD in Figure 10.22.

```
Tim World                                    0/25
Tim's awesome Minecraft Server!
```

FIGURE 10.22 A customized server icon and MOTD make your server "pop" in your players' multiplayer server list.

Final Thoughts

Wow—can you believe it? We've come to the end of the road. How was the journey for you? I hope you know more about Minecraft server administration than you did before you started reading this book! If so, I did my job.

I look forward to visiting your Minecraft server! Let's stay in touch: You can reach me directly at timothywarner316@gmail.com. Thanks so much for taking the time to study this book, and I wish you all the best in life. Take care, and happy Minecrafting!

Appendix

Tim's "Top 10" Lists

If you're anything like me, then you've read this book all the way through and are now ready to apply your knowledge. But wait—what was the name of that modpack again? Who did Tim say were the most reliable Minecraft hosting companies in his opinion?

You get the idea. I'm closing my book by giving you a sequence of (admittedly subjective) "top 10" lists that allow you to quickly find those bits of information you need without necessarily rereading part of a chapter. Now, please understand that the word *subjective* is operative here. Specifically, I want you to keep the following two points in mind as you read my lists:

- These suggestions spring from my personal experiences and research; use them or throw them away to suit your preferences and your own opinions.

- I intentionally put each "top 10" list in an unordered format to denote that I'm not classifying my lists in any particular numerical ranking order.

You'll note that I've used the Bitly.com URL shortening service to make these web addresses easier to transcribe into your browser. Don't forget that the last part of these URLs is case sensitive. In other words, the URL http://bit.ly/1GtZT82 is totally different from, say, http://bit.ly/1gtzt82.

Alrighty then! With that explanatory and disclaimer information out of the way, let's get to the lists themselves! I hope that you find that this material saves you time in developing the Minecraft server(s) of your dreams. Good luck!

Top 10 Minecraft Hosts

A Minecraft hosting company rents space in its data center to you so you can host Minecraft multiplayer games without having to worry about the hassle and security issues associated with personal hosting.

Many Minecraft hosts use the Multicraft control panel (http://bit.ly/1B60EBU); I show you part of that interface in Figure A.1.

- MCProHosting (http://bit.ly/1B604Es)

- Beastnode (http://bit.ly/1B5ZiY7)

- CubedHost (http://bit.ly/1B60ieG)

- NodeCraft (http://bit.ly/1B60t9Y)

- BisectHosting (http://bit.ly/1B60z19)

- EnviousHost (http://bit.ly/1B60xXf)

- CreeperHost (http://bit.ly/1B60ESz)

- Fragnet (http://bit.ly/1B60F96)

- GGServers (http://bit.ly/1B60D0O)

- Nitrous Networks (http://bit.ly/1B60FWD)

FIGURE A.1 The Multicraft Control Panel is pretty standard for Minecraft hosting providers.

Top 10 Public Minecraft Servers

Many Minecraft fans get into hosting their own servers only after spending lots of time on other, public servers, and figuring out which features they like or don't like.

The biggest and most popular Minecraft servers have the resources to develop highly sophisticated community websites. For instance, take a look at TheArchon server's front page, as shown in Figure A.2.

- Mineplex (http://bit.ly/1B61cIf)
- Hypixel (http://bit.ly/1B61fDG)
- Lichcraft (http://bit.ly/1B61fUl)
- TheArchon (http://bit.ly/1B61izo)
- MythCraft (http://bit.ly/1B61oqQ)
- PixelmonCraft (http://bit.ly/1B61s9X)
- Dreamcraft (http://bit.ly/1B61sHb)
- FadeCloud (http://bit.ly/1B61vme)
- Cube Craft Games (http://bit.ly/1B61yyy)
- MC-Legends (http://bit.ly/1B61tdW)

FIGURE A.2   TheArchon server's front page.

Top 10 Bukkit Plugins

Although the status of the Minecraft plugin ecosystem remains in heavy flux at the time of this writing, you can still get a lot of mileage out of the Bukkit architecture.

For instance, Figure A.3 shows some of the in-game player experience featured in the DonationCraft plugin. With DonationCraft, you can deploy professional stores, both inside and outside your multiplayer worlds.

- WorldEdit (http://bit.ly/1B61PRU)
- ClearLagg (http://bit.ly/1B61Ntr)
- PermissionsEx (http://bit.ly/1B61QoV)
- WorldGuard (http://bit.ly/1B61TB6)
- Essentials (http://bit.ly/1B61TRE)
- CraftBukkitUpToDate (http://bit.ly/1B61RsX)
- Multiverse (http://bit.ly/1B61U8m)
- GroupManager (http://bit.ly/1B61RZW)
- DonationCraft (http://bit.ly/1B61SNL)
- Votifier (http://bit.ly/1B61VZP)

FIGURE A.3   The DonationCraft plugin in action.

Top 10 Modpacks

Modpacks can change your Minecraft worlds from proverbial top to bottom. For instance, my five-year-old daughter Zoey loves Pokémon; by installing Pixelmon, we can have the best of both worlds (pun intended).

Figure A.4 shows an ore processing facility from a Hexxit-equipped public Minecraft server.

- Feed the Beast (http://bit.ly/1B62OBA)
- Direwolf20 (http://bit.ly/1B62RgW)
- Agrarian Skies 2 (http://bit.ly/1B62Ut1)
- Tekkit (http://bit.ly/1B62V02)
- Pixelmon (http://bit.ly/1B62XF6)
- Hexxit (http://bit.ly/1B62XVz)
- Combat Pack (http://bit.ly/1B62YJf)
- Magic Farm 3: Harvest (http://bit.ly/1B630kc)
- Atonement: Sins of the Past (http://bit.ly/1B633ww)
- Crash Landing (http://bit.ly/1B630AK)

FIGURE A.4 Hexxit both broadens and deepens Minecraft's default environment.

Top 10 Resource/Texture Packs

Whereas a modpack completely transforms your Minecraft worlds, *resource packs* (also called texture packs) are used to modify only parts of your worlds. For instance, Figure A.5 show-cases Xray Ultimate, which makes it a snap to see through blocks to discover where all the valuable ore lies.

- Faithful 32x32 (http://bit.ly/1B63eI8)
- Soartex Fanver (http://bit.ly/1B63Jlq)
- Xray Ultimate (http://bit.ly/1B63mr3)
- MarioKart (http://bit.ly/1B63K94)
- Soartex Invictus (http://bit.ly/1B63Ihv)
- Pixel Perfection (http://bit.ly/1B63NBQ)
- Runescape Pack (http://bit.ly/1B63U0c)
- Equanimity (http://bit.ly/1B63Tcz)
- John Smith Legacy (http://bit.ly/1B63PcW)
- Default HD (http://bit.ly/1B63Q0s)

FIGURE A.5 Make your ore mining much faster and more accurate by installing Xray Ultimate.

Top 10 Minecraft YouTubers

The YouTubers in this list all make enough money via advertising revenue that they can (and often do) make recording Minecraft "Let's Play" videos their full-time job. Because my daughter Zoey loves Stampy, I shared a picture of his avatar in Figure A.6.

- SkyDoesMinecraft (http://bit.ly/1dYC7OH)
- The Syndicate Project (http://bit.ly/1gRpf0U)
- Stampy (http://bit.ly/1B64gUG)
- CaptainSparklez (http://bit.ly/1B64jzF)
- TheBajanCanadian (http://bit.ly/1B64mvv)
- JeromeASF (http://bit.ly/1B64oDz)
- AntVenom (http://bit.ly/1B64pHM)
- TheDiamondMinecart (http://bit.ly/1B64rPN)
- Popular MMOs (http://bit.ly/1B64sTV)
- SSundee (http://bit.ly/1B64HhI)

FIGURE A.6 Stampy Cat is Stampy's (Joseph Garrett's) in-world avatar.

Top 10 Minecraft Minigames

Minigames give server operators and their players an opportunity to "mix it up" and approach the game outside the typical mining and crafting fare. I show you a Prison game as a representative example in Figure A.7.

- Parkour (http://bit.ly/1B65DTf)
- Skyblock (http://bit.ly/1B65E9M)

- PvP (http://bit.ly/1B65E9V)
- Spleef (http://bit.ly/1B65Gi2)
- Survival Games (http://bit.ly/1B65Gyt)
- Cops & Robbers (http://bit.ly/1B65EGR)
- Prison (http://bit.ly/1B65KhH)
- Faction (http://bit.ly/1B65Ky5)
- Skywars (http://bit.ly/1B65Kyg)
- Economy (http://bit.ly/1B65K19)

FIGURE A.7 In the Prison minigame, you're either a jailer or an escape-minded prisoner.

Top 10 Minecraft Custom Maps

What's great about Minecraft custom maps is that you can save yourself hours of work when you're designing your multiplayer worlds. For example, check out Figure A.8, which shows part of the TolkienCraft II map.

- WesterosCraft (http://bit.ly/1B67esh)
- Assassin's Creep (http://bit.ly/1B673Nx)
- Herobrine's Mansion (http://bit.ly/1B671VW)
- Diversity 2 (http://bit.ly/1B67abV)
- TolkienCraft II (http://bit.ly/1B66VgY)

- Agrarian Skies 2 (http://bit.ly/1B67ckd)
- Stampy World (http://bit.ly/1B6797O)
- Minevolution (http://bit.ly/1B670RW)
- Hotel Paradise (http://bit.ly/1B66SSI)
- Micro Cubes (http://bit.ly/1B66Ny4)

FIGURE A.8 The TolkienCraft Minecraft map puts Middle Earth within your reach.

Top 10 Minecraft Seeds

A Minecraft world seed is an integer value that represents the starting point for a world. Enter the seed ID value in your Minecraft client's Create New World screen, and off you go! I show you an underwater temple in Figure A.9.

- Spawn Beside Jungle Temple (3083175)
- Stronghold in Ravine (7352190906321318631)
- Village with Lots of Loot (-516687594611420526)
- Underwater Temple (-7185414603555797276)
- Diamond Desert Temple (-4213002892151667621)
- Floating Island (68063653)
- Close-Together Biomes (-8913466909937400889)

- Mega Mountains (3657966)
- Nether Fortress (6890863638126214101)
- Swamp and Witch Hut (2020)

FIGURE A.9   Minecraft seeds put you right in the middle of any action you're interested in.

INDEX

A

@a target selector, 151

Absolute Beginner's Guide to Minecraft Mods Programming (Cadenhead), 26

accessing multiplayer game, 6

accounts, BuyCraft, 220-223

Adams, Scott, 25

AdCraft, 217

addresses

connection addresses, 15

IP addresses

banning, 62

DHCP (Dynamic Host Configuration Protocol), 75

explained, 73-74

finding, 39

hostnames versus, 88

IPv4 versus IPv6, 78

mapping to hostnames, 88-90

NAT (Network Address Translation), 75

public versus private addresses, 74-75

AdF.ly Skipper extension, 189

The Advanced Strategy Guide to Minecraft (O'Brien), 122

Adventure mode, 6

Adventurize web portal, 217

advertising, 228

in-game advertising and sponsorship, 216-217

on Minecraft server lists, 228-229

server registration, 231

server status banners, 229-231

voting, 232

Agrarian Skies 2, 241, 245

agreeing to EULA, 34-35

Alexander, Scott, 209

allow-flight property, 50

allow-nether property, 49

Anarchy minigame, 14

Angelou, Maya, 93

Announcement, 213-214

announce-player-achievements property, 49

AntVenom, 243

%appdata% variable, 123

APIs (application programming interfaces)

  BukGet, 172

  Minecraft Forge

    explained, 114

    installing, 115-116

application programming interfaces. *See* APIs

Assassin's Creep, 244

Asterion Minecraft, 135

ATLauncher, 134-135

Atonement: Sins of the Past, 241

attacks

  DDoS (distributed denial-of-service) attacks, 186-188

  DoS (denial-of-service) attacks, 186

  grief protection

    blocking griefers, 190-194

    hacking yourself, 189

    overview, 188

    tips for addressing griefers, 194

auto-afk (Essentials plugin), 107

auto-afk-kick (Essentials plugin), 107

autocomplete, 57

availability of third-party hosts, 162

B

backups, Minecraft Realms

  forcing, 155

  viewing, 154

/ban command, 61-63, 192

/ban-ip command, 61-63, 192

banners, server status banners, 229-231

basic servers. *See* vanilla servers

BeastNode, 183, 238

Berra, Yogi, 45

BisectHosting, 183, 238

blacklist (Essentials plugin), 108

blocking griefers, 190-194

blocks (command)

  explained, 150

  programming, 152-153

  target selectors, 151

BuildCraft, 122

BuildTools instructions, 95

BukGet, 172

Bukkit

  history of, 93-94

  plugins. *See* plugins

BukkitWiki, 98

bukkit.yml file, 98

BungeeCord, 208

BuyCraft, 212, 220

  creating BuyCraft account, 220-223

  creating free packages, 226-227

  creating paid packages, 223-225

  giving paid item to all players, 225

buying Minecraft license, 7-8, 34

Buy Realms Subscription page (Minecraft Realms), 140

C

Cadenhead, Rogers, 26

CaptainSparklez, 243

Capture the Flag minigame, 14

Cauldron

  explained, 113-114

  installing, 117

chat

  chat window, clearing, 57

  console commands for, 55-58

  MCProHosting, 174

  in multiplayer game, 20-23

chat window, clearing, 57

choosing third-party host, 161-162

Chrome, 100, 189

City minigame, 14

clearing chat window, 57

ClearLagg, 101, 240

client mods, 135

clients

  client mods, 135

  client/server applications, 22

  defined, 22

  Forge client

    explained, 114

    installing, 115-116

client/server applications, 22

Close-Together Biomes, 245

CloudFlare, 188

cloud services

  advantages/disadvantages, 139

  explained, 137-139

Minecraft Realms

  backups, 154-155

  creating realms, 142-144

  explained, 139-140

  inviting players, 145-147

  managing players, 148-150

  restoring worlds, 157

  subscribing to, 140-141

  uploading worlds to, 156-157

Combat Pack, 241

command blocks, 57

  explained, 150

  programming, 152-153

  target selectors, 151

command-costs (Essentials plugin), 107

console commands

  /ban, 192

  /ban-i, 192

  for chat messages, 55-58

  Essentials plugin, 112

  /gamerule, 148

  /give, 150

  for giving items, 59

  /kick, 192

  /list, 148

  list of, 56

  /mvp, 205

  pl, 120

  for player discipline, 59-64

  /setworldspawn, 148

in SpigotMC, 96

/summon, 148

for teleportation, 59

/time, 148

/toggledownfall, 148

for vanilla servers, 37-42

config files

editing on MCProHosting, 175-176

for vanilla servers, 35-37

Configure Realm screen (Minecraft Realms), 145

configuring

Essentials plugin, 106-108

Minecraft server on MCProHosting, 169-170

port forwarding, 83-85

SpigotMC, 97-98

config.yml file, 106-108

connecting multiple worlds, 206-207

connection addresses, 15

console commands. *See* commands

Control Panel (MCProHosting), 168-169

Cops & Robbers, 14, 244

CoreProtect, 192

cosmetic upgrade sales, 217-219

cracked launchers, avoiding, 8-9

CraftBukkit, 93-94

CraftBukkitUpToDate, 240

Crash Landing, 241

Create Realm button (Minecraft Realms), 144

Creative mode, 6

CreeperHost, 183, 238

Cube Craft Games, 239

CubedHost, 238

Cubeville, 233-234

currency-symbol (Essentials plugin), 107

custom-join-message (Essentials plugin), 107

custom maps, 244-245

custom-quit-message (Essentials plugin), 107

custom server entries, creating, 234

custom servers. *See* plugins

Bukkit/CraftBukkit, 93-94

Cauldron

explained, 113-114

installing, 117

SpigotMC

changing version numbers, 104-105

configuring, 97-98

installing, 95-96

reasons for using, 94

starting, 96-97

testing player experience, 99-100

D

day/night cycle, 40

DDNS (Dynamic Domain Name System), 88

DDoS (distributed denial-of-service) attacks, 186-188

debug window, opening, 59

dedicated servers, 161

Default HD, 242

default port numbers, 81-83

demo copy limitations, 7

denial-of-service (DoS) attacks, 186

deploying

portals, 203-205

resource packs with MCProHosting, 177-180

DHCP (Dynamic Host Configuration Protocol), 75

Diamond Desert Temple, 245

difficulty property, 49

Direwolf20, 241

Direwolf server, 132

disciplining players, console commands for, 59-64

distributed denial-of-service (DDoS) attacks, 186-188

Diversity 2, 244

DNS (Domain Name System), 88

domain name mapping, 180-182

Domain Name System (DNS), 88

DonationCraft, 240

donations, soliciting, 212-216

DoS (denial-of-service) attacks, 186

downloading

FTB (Feed the Beast), 130

JRE (Java Runtime Environment), 27-28

PEX (PermissionsEx) plugin, 118

Dreamcraft, 239

Dropbox, 177

Dynamic Domain Name System (DDNS), 88

Dynamic Host Configuration Protocol (DHCP), 75

Dyn (hostname service), 88

E

@e target selector, 151

Economy, 14, 244

editing config files on MCProHosting, 175-176

editions of McMyAdmin, 68

enable-command-block property, 49

enable-query property, 49

enable-rcon property, 50

end user license agreement (EULA), 11, 210-211

agreeing for vanilla servers, 34-35

for Minecraft servers, 10

Engineering with Minecraft (Kelly), 196

EnviousHost, 238

Equanimity, 242

errors. *See* troubleshooting

Essentials, 101, 240

configuring, 106-108

installing, 102-105

testing player experience, 108-112

Essentials Wiki, 112

EULA (end user license agreement), 11, 210-211

agreeing for vanilla servers, 34-35

for Minecraft servers, 10

extensions for Google Chrome, 100

F

Faction, 14, 244

FadeCloud, 239

Faithful 32x32, 177, 242

Feed the Beast (FTB), 14, 241

downloading, 130

installing FTB server, 132-133

setting up, 130-131

starting FTB launcher, 134

file extensions, viewing, 31

finding

IP addresses, 39

item IDs, 59

online servers

connection addresses, 15

EULA stipulations, 10-11

Minecraft Forum, 11-14

public versus whitelist servers, 15-16

vanilla servers online, 43-44

version numbers in SpigotMC, 99-100

firewalls, 81

flexibility of third-party hosts, 162

Floating Island, 245

force-gamemode property, 49

forcing Minecraft Realms backups, 155

Forge client

explained, 114

installing, 115-116

FQDN (fully qualified domain name), 88

Fragnet, 238

free packages, creating, 226-227

FTB (Feed the Beast), 14, 241

downloading, 130

installing FTB server, 132-133

setting up, 130-131

starting FTB launcher, 134

fully qualified domain name (FQDN), 88

G

gamemode property, 49

/gamerule console command, 40

/gamerule doDaylightCycle false command, 148

gaming experience, improving, 185

multiple worlds

connecting, 206-207

Multiverse Core, 202-203

Multiverse Portals, 202

portal deployment, 203-205

teleporting between, 203

server protection

DDoS (distributed denial-of-service) attacks, 186-188

grief protection, 188-194

motivations of server abusers, 186

world spawn, 194

  building spawn lobbies, 196-198

  setting server spawn, 195

  WorldEdit, 199-201

Gandhi, Mahatma, 185

generate-structures property, 50

generator-settings property, 49

generic servers. *See* vanilla servers

Get Realms button (Minecraft Realms), 140

GGServers, 183, 238

GigaTech, 135

/give command, 59, 150

GiveAllItems Bukkit plugin, 225

giving items

  console commands for, 59

  giving paid items to all players, 225

GoDaddy, 180-182

Google Chrome, 100, 189

griefing, 15, 59-60

grief protection

  blocking griefers, 190-194

  hacking yourself, 189

  overview, 188

  tips for addressing griefers, 194

GroupManager, 240

H

hacking yourself, 189

hacktivism, 186

Hardcore mode, 6

hardcore property, 49

Hardcore PvP minigame, 14

/help console command, 19-20, 37

help system in multiplayer game, 19-20

Herobrine's Mansion, 244

Hexxit, 241

history of Bukkit/CraftBukkit, 93-94

hostnames, 88

  DNS (Domain Name System), 88

  No-IP configuration, 88-90

hosts, top 10 Minecraft hosts, 237-238

Hotel Paradise, 245

Hunger Games minigame, 14

Hypixel, 239

I

identity theft, 186

improving gaming experience, 185

  multiple worlds

    connecting, 206-207

    Multiverse Core, 202-203

    Multiverse Portals, 202

    portal deployment, 203-205

    teleporting between, 203

  server protection

    DDoS (distributed denial-of-service) attacks, 186-188

    grief protection, 188-194

    motivations of server abusers, 186

world spawn, 194

building spawn lobbies, 196-198

setting server spawn, 195

WorldEdit, 199-201

IndustrialCraft2, 122

in-game advertising and sponsorship, 216-217

installing

Cauldron, 117

Forge client, 115-116

FTB (Feed the Beast) server, 132-133

JRE (Java Runtime Environment), 27-28

McMyAdmin, 66

Minecraft, 8

mods, 122-123

plugins

Essentials plugin, 102-105

MCProHosting, 172-173

number to install, 102

Railcraft, 122-123

SpigotMC, 95-96

vanilla servers

on Mac OS X, 31-33

on Windows, 29-30

Internet Protocol (IP) addresses. *See* IP addresses

Intreppid, 186

inviting players in Minecraft Realms, 145-147

IP addresses

banning, 62

DHCP (Dynamic Host Configuration Protocol), 75

explained, 73-74

finding, 39

hostnames versus, 88

IPv4 versus IPv6, 78

mapping to hostnames, 88-90

NAT (Network Address Translation), 75

public versus private addresses, 74-75

IPv4 addresses, 78

IPv6 addresses, 78

item IDs, finding, 59

item-spawn-blacklist (Essentials plugin), 107

J

Java environment preparation, 25

JRE installation, 27-28

verifying Java version, 26-27

Java Runtime Environment (JRE), 27-28

JavaScript Object Notation (JSON), 37

java - version command errors, 27

JeromeASF, 243

John Smith Legacy, 242

joining

MCProHosting, 163-168

online servers, 16-19

JRE (Java Runtime Environment), 27-28

JSON (JavaScript Object Notation), 37

K

Kelly, James Floyd, 196

/kick command, 60-61, 192

kit:tools (Essentials plugin), 108

kits (Essentials plugin), 107

L

LAN (local area network) servers

  defined, 10

  opening single-player game to, 68-70

  user connections, 50-52

launchers

  Asterion Minecraft, 135

  ATLauncher, 134-135

  avoiding cracked, 8-9

  FTB (Feed the Beast) launcher, 134

  GigaTech, 135

  TechnicPack, 135

  VoidLauncher, 135

level-name property, 50

level-seed property, 50

level-type property, 49

license for Minecraft, buying, 7-8, 34

Lichcraft, 239

/list command, 21, 148

lists, advertising on, 228-229

lobbies (spawn), building, 196-198

local area network (LAN) servers

  defined, 10

  opening single-player game to, 68-70

  user connections, 50-52

location coordinates, 59

logfiles, reading, 52-54

logging in to MCProHosting, 170-171

M

Mac OS X

  finding IP addresses, 39

  startup scripts, 96

  TCP/IP configuration settings, 77

  vanilla server installation, 31-33

  verifying Java version, 27

  viewing file extensions, 31

Magic Farm 3: Harvest, 241

managing

  players in Minecraft Realms, 148-150

  vanilla servers with McMyAdmin, 65-68

Manneh, Carl, 137, 157

mapping

  hostnames to IP addresses, 88-90

  servers to domains, 180-182

maps, top 10 Minecraft custom maps, 244-245

MarioKart, 242

max-build-height property, 50

max-players property, 49

max-tick-time property, 49

max-world-size property, 49

MCEdit, 197-198

MC-Legends, 239

McMyAdmin, 65-68

MCProHosting, 238

chat, 174

configuring and starting Minecraft server, 169-170

Control Panel, 168-169

deploying resource packs, 177-180

domain name mapping, 180-182

editing config files, 175-176

installing plugins, 172-173

joining, 163-168

logging in, 170-171

MCSchematics, 197

/me console command, 58

Mega Mountains, 246

message of the day (MOTD), 235

Micro Cubes, 245

Microsoft's purchase of Mojang, 211

Minecraft EULA (end user license agreement), 210-211

Minecraft Forge

explained, 114

installing, 115-116

Minecraft Forum, 11-14, 184

Minecraft hosts, 237-238

Minecraftopia, 59

Minecraft Realms, 10

backups

forcing, 155

viewing, 154

creating realms, 142-144

explained, 139-140

inviting players, 145-147

managing players, 148-150

restoring worlds, 157

subscribing to, 140-141

uploading worlds to, 156-157

Minecraft Schematics, 197

Minecraft seeds, 245-246

Minecraft server lists, advertising on, 228-229

Minecraft Wiki, 56

Mineplex, 239

Minevolution, 245

minigames, 14-15, 243-244

modpacks

BuildCraft, 122

FTB (Feed the Beast), 14, 241

downloading, 130

installing FTB server, 132-133

setting up, 130-131

starting FTB launcher, 134

IndustrialCraft2, 122

launchers, 134-135

Pixelmon, 122

Railcraft

explained, 122

installing, 122-123

testing, 125-129

Tinkers Construct, 122

top 10 modpacks, 240-241

mods, 113, 122

BuildCraft, 122

Cauldron project, 113-114

client mods, 135

FTB (Feed the Beast), 14, 241
  downloading, 130
  installing FTB server, 132-133
  setting up, 130-131
  starting FTB launcher, 134
IndustrialCraft2, 122
launchers, 134-135
Minecraft Forge
  explained, 114
  installing, 115-116
Optifine, 135
Pixelmon, 122
plugins versus, 100
programming, 26
Railcraft
  explained, 122
  installing, 122-123
  testing, 125-129
Rei's Minimap, 135
Tekkit, 122
Tinkers Construct, 122
TooManyItems, 135
monetizing Minecraft server
  advertising your server
    on Minecraft server lists, 228-229
    server registration, 231
    server status banners, 229-231
    voting, 232
  BuyCraft
    creating BuyCraft account, 220-223
    creating free packages, 226-227
    creating paid packages, 223-225
    giving paid item to all players, 225

  cosmetic upgrade sales, 217-219
  Cubeville example, 233-234
  custom server entries, 234
  donations, 212-216
  in-game advertising and sponsorship, 216-217
  Minecraft EULA (end user license agreement), 210-211
  Mojang's position on, 210
  MOTD (message of the day), 235
  overview, 209
  VIP server access/subscriptions, 219-220
MOTD (message of the day), 235
motd property, 50
motivations of server abusers, 186
Multicraft, 162
multiplayer game
  accessing, 6
  chatting in, 20-23
  defined, 10
  game types, 10
  help system, 19-20
  minigames, 14-15
  netiquette, 19, 23-24
  opening single-player game as, 68-70
multiple server instances, running, 42-43
multiple worlds
  connecting, 206-207
  Multiverse Core, 202-203
  Multiverse Portals, 202

portal deployment, 203-205

teleporting between, 203

Multiverse, 240

Multiverse Core, 102, 202-203

Multiverse Portals, 202

/mvp command, 205

MythCraft, 239

N

NAT (Network Address Translation), 75

Nether Fortress, 246

netiquette in multiplayer game, 19, 23-24

Network Address Translation (NAT), 75

network-compression-threshold property, 49

networks

DHCP (Dynamic Host Configuration Protocol), 75

firewalls, 81

hostnames

DNS (Domain Name System), 88

No-IP configuration, 88-90

IP addresses

banning, 62

DHCP (Dynamic Host Configuration Protocol), 75

explained, 73-74

finding, 39

hostnames versus, 88

IPv4 versus IPv6, 78

mapping to hostnames, 88-90

NAT (Network Address Translation), 75

public versus private addresses, 74-75

NAT (Network Address Translation), 75

port forwarding

configuring, 83-85

explained, 81-83

testing, 85-87

port numbers, 81-83

router configuration settings, 78-80

security issues, 90-91

TCP/IP configuration settings, 76-78

terminology, 73

topology, 72

Nitrous Networks, 238

NoCheatPlus, 190

NodeCraft, 238

Nodus, 188

No-IP (hostname service), 88-90

O

O'Brien, Stephen, 122

online-mode property, 50

online servers

defined, 10

finding

connection addresses, 15

EULA stipulations, 10-11

Minecraft Forum, 11-14

public versus whitelist servers, 15-16

vanilla servers, 43-44

joining, 16-19

on-premises services, 137

/op console command, 38

opening

debug window, 59

single-player game as multiplayer, 68-70

op-permission-level property, 49

OPs, 22

ops-name-color (Essentials plugin), 107

Optifine, 135

OS X. *See* Mac OS X

Ownage Hosting, 183

P

@p target selector, 151

packages, creating

free packages, 226-227

paid packages, 223-225

paid items, giving to all players, 225

paid packages, creating, 223-225

/pardon console command, 63-64

/pardon-ip console command, 63-64

Parkour, 14, 243

passwords, 80

Perlis, Alan, 71

PermissionsEx (PEX) plugin, 240

downloading, 118

quick start, 118-120

testing, 120-121

PermissionsEx plugin, 101

PEX (PermissionsEx) plugin, 240

downloading, 118

quick start, 118-120

testing, 120-121

Pixelmon, 122, 241

PixelmonCraft, 239

Pixel Perfection, 242

player connections to vanilla servers, 86-87

player experience, testing

Essentials plugin, 108-112

in SpigotMC, 99-100

player-idle-timeout property, 49

player interactions

chat messages, 55-58

disciplining players, 59-64

giving items, 59

inviting in Minecraft Realms, 145-147

managing in Minecraft Realms, 148-150

teleportation, 59

player list, viewing, 56

Player versus Environment (PvE) minigame, 15

Player versus Player (PvP) minigame, 14

pl command, 120

plugins

AdCraft, 217

Announcement, 213-214

BuyCraft. *See* BuyCraft

configuring, 106-108

defined, 100

GiveAllItems, 225

installing, 102-105

MCProHosting, 172-173

mods versus, 100

most popular, 100-102

NoCheatPlus, 190

number to install, 102

PEX (PermissionsEx)

  downloading, 118

  quick start, 118-120

  testing, 120-121

  testing player experience, 108-112

  top 10 Bukkit plugins, 240

  VIP, 219-220

Popular MMOs, 243

portals, deploying, 203-205

PortCheckTool.com, 85

port forwarding

  configuring, 83-85

  explained, 81-83

  testing, 85-87

port numbers, 81-83

prevent:spawn (Essentials plugin), 107

Prison, 15, 244

privacy issues, 76

private IP addresses, 74-75

programming mods, 26

programming command blocks, 152-153

protecting servers, 186

  DDoS (distributed denial-of-service) attacks, 186-188

grief protection

  blocking griefers, 190-194

  hacking yourself, 189

  overview, 188

  tips for addressing griefers, 194

  motivations of server abusers, 186

proxies, 208

public IP addresses, 74-75

public servers

  top 10 servers, 239

  whitelist servers versus, 15-16

purchasing Minecraft license, 7-8, 34

PvP, 244

pvp property, 49

Q-R

@r target selector, 151

Railcraft

  explained, 122

  installing, 122-123

  testing, 125-129

rain, starting/stopping, 40

RAM (random access memory) system requirements, 34

reading logfiles, 52-54

Realms, 10

  backups

    forcing, 155

    viewing, 154

  creating realms, 142-144

  explained, 139-140

  inviting players, 145-147

managing players, 148-150

restoring worlds, 157

subscribing to, 140-141

uploading worlds to, 156-157

Realm Templates screen (Minecraft Realms), 144

Reddit MinecraftSchematics, 197

registering servers, 231

Rei's Minimap, 135

repositories

  Bukkit plugins, 100

  Essentials plugin, 102

reputation of third-party hosts, 161

resource-pack-hash property, 49

resource-pack property, 50

resource packs

  deploying with MCProHosting, 177-180

  top 10 resource packs, 242

restoring worlds in Minecraft Realms, 157

router configuration settings, 78-80

routers, port forwarding

  configuring, 83-85

  testing, 85-87

Runescape Pack, 242

running multiple server instances, 42-43

Russell, Bertrand, 113

S

/say console command, 40, 55

schematics, 197-198

  popular schematic sites, 197

  preparing land for, 197

  with MCEdit, 197-198

  with WorldEdit, 199-201

security, 186

  DDoS (distributed denial-of-service) attacks, 186-188

  grief protection

    blocking griefers, 190-194

    hacking yourself, 189

    overview, 188

    tips for addressing griefers, 194

  motivations of server abusers, 186

  network services, 90-91

  routers, 80

  vanilla servers, warning about, 76

seeds, 245-246

Select Template button (Minecraft Realms), 144

server console, 53

server-ip property, 50

server monetization

  advertising your server

    on Minecraft server lists, 228-229

    server registration, 231

    server status banners, 229-231

    voting, 232

  BuyCraft

    creating BuyCraft account, 220-223

    creating free packages, 226-227

    creating paid packages, 223-225

    giving paid item to all players, 225

  cosmetic upgrade sales, 217-219

  Cubeville example, 233-234

custom server entries, 234

donations, 212-216

in-game advertising and sponsorship, 216-217

Minecraft EULA (end user license agreement), 210-211

Mojang's position on, 210

MOTD (message of the day), 235

overview, 209

VIP server access/subscriptions, 219-220

server-port property, 50

server.properties file

configuring SpigotMC, 98

settings, 48-50

server registration, 231

servers

custom servers

Bukkit/CraftBukkit history, 93-94

Cauldron, 113-114, 117

changing version numbers, 104-105

installing SpigotMC, 95-100

dedicated servers, 161

defined, 22

Direwolf, 132

FTB (Feed the Beast) server, installing, 132-133

LAN servers

defined, 10

opening single-player game to, 68-70

mapping to domains, 180-182

Minecraft Realms, 10

monetization

advertising your server, 228-232

BuyCraft, 220-227

cosmetic upgrade sales, 217-219

Cubeville example, 233-234

custom server entries, 234

donations, 212-216

in-game advertising and sponsorship, 216-217

Minecraft EULA (end user license agreement), 210-211

Mojang's position on, 210

MOTD (message of the day), 235

overview, 209

VIP server access/subscriptions, 219-220

online servers

connection addresses, 15

defined, 10

EULA stipulations, 10-11

finding, 11-14

joining, 16-19

public versus whitelist servers, 15-16

protecting

DDoS (distributed denial-of-service) attacks, 186-188

grief protection, 188-194

motivations of server abusers, 186

registering, 231

system requirements, 34

top 10 public Minecraft servers, 239

uptimes, 13

vanilla servers

advantages/disadvantages, 28-29

agreeing to EULA, 34-35

chat messages, 55-58

configuration files, 35-37

console commands, 37-42

finding online, 43-44

giving items, 59

installing on Mac OS X, 31-33

installing on Windows, 29-30

Java environment preparation, 25-28

logfiles, 53-54

managing with McMyAdmin, 65-68

mapping IP address to hostname, 88-90

meaning of term, 28, 34

player connections, 86-87

player discipline, 59-64

port forwarding configuration, 83-85

running multiple instances, 42-43

security, 90-91

security issues, 76

server console UI, 53

server.properties file settings, 48-50

teleportation, 59

test environment, 45-46

testing port forwarding, 85-87

user connections via LAN, 50-52

UUIDs, 53-55

VPSs (virtual private servers), 160

server specifications (third-party hosts), 161

server status banners, 229-231

services

cloud services. See also Minecraft Realms

advantages/disadvantages, 139

explained, 137-139

on-premises services, 137

third-party hosting

BeastNode, 183

Bisect Hosting, 183

choosing hosts, 161-162

Creeper Host, 183

dedicated servers, 161

GGServers, 183

MCProHosting, 163-182

overview, 159

Ownage Hosting, 183

VPSs (virtual private servers), 160

/setworldspawn command, 148

showing. See viewing

signing up with Minecraft Realms, 140-141

signs (Essentials plugin), 107

single-player game

modes of play, 6

opening to multiplayer, 68-70

Skyblock, 15, 243

SkyDoesMinecraft, 243

Skywars, 244

snooper-enabled property, 49

Soartex Fanver, 242

Soartex Invictus, 242

soliciting donations, 212-216

spawn-animals property, 50

Spawn Beside Jungle Temple, 245

spawn lobbies, building, 196-198

spawn-monsters property, 49

spawn-npcs property, 50

spawn-protection property, 48

Spectator mode, 6

SpigotMC

    changing version numbers, 104-105

    configuring, 97-98

    installing, 95-96

    reasons for using, 94

    starting, 96-97

    testing player experience, 99-100

SpigotMC Wiki, 98

spigot.yml file, 98

Spleef, 244

sponsorship, 216-217

SSundee, 243

Stampy, 243

Stampy Cat, 209

stampylonghead YouTube channel, 209

Stampy World, 245

starting

    FTB (Feed the Beast) launcher, 134

    Minecraft server on MCProHosting, 169-170

    SpigotMC, 96-97

starting-balance (Essentials plugin), 107

startup scripts, creating, 96

status banners, 229-231

/stop console command, 40-42

Stronghold in Ravine, 245

Sublime Text, 47-48

subnet masks, 73-74

subscribing to Minecraft Realms, 140-141

/summon command, 148

Sun Tzu, 5

Survival Games, 244

Survival mode, 6

Swamp and Witch Hut, 246

The Syndicate Project, 243

system requirements

    for McMyAdmin, 67

    for Minecraft, 7

    for servers, 34

T

Tab key

    autocomplete, 57

    viewing player list, 56

target selectors, 151

TCP/IP (Transmission Control Protocol/Internet Protocol), 73, 76-78

TechnicPack, 135

Tekkit, 15, 122, 241

teleportation

    console commands for, 59

    teleporting between worlds, 203

teleport-cooldown (Essentials plugin), 107

/tell console command, 20, 57

terminology for networks, 73

testing

    Essentials plugin, 108-112

    PEX (PermissionsEx) plugin, 120-121

player experience in SpigotMC, 99-100

port forwarding, 85-87

Railcraft, 125-129

test environment for vanilla servers, 45-46

text editors, Sublime Text, 47-48

texture packs, 242

TheArchon, 239

TheBajanCanadian, 243

TheDiamondMinecart, 243

third-party hosting

  BeastNode, 183

  Bisect Hosting, 183

  choosing hosts, 161-162

  Creeper Host, 183

  dedicated servers, 161

  GGServers, 183

  MCProHosting

    chat, 174

    configuring and starting Minecraft server, 169-170

    Control Panel, 168-169

    deploying resource packs, 177-180

    domain name mapping, 180-182

    editing config files, 175-176

    installing plugins, 172-173

    joining, 163-168

    logging in, 170-171

  overview, 159

  Ownage Hosting, 183

  VPSs (virtual private servers), 160

/time console command, 40

/time set day 1000 command, 148

Tinkers Construct, 122

/toggledownfall command, 40, 148

TolkienCraft II, 244

TooManyItems, 135

Top 10 lists, 237

  Bukkit plugins, 240

  custom maps, 244-245

  Minecraft hosts, 237-238

  Minecraft seeds, 245-246

  Minecraft YouTubers, 243

  minigames, 243-244

  modpacks, 240-241

  public Minecraft servers, 239

  resource packs, 242

topology of networks, 72

TownCraft, 194

/tp console command, 59

Transmission Control Protocol/Internet Protocol (TCP/IP), 73

troubleshooting

  java - version command errors, 27

  port forwarding errors, 86

  SpigotMC console commands, 96

  typos, 33

typos, 33

U

UI (user interface) for server console, 53

Underwater Temple, 245

universally unique identifiers (UUIDs), 53-55

uploading worlds to Minecraft Realms, 156-157

uptimes for servers, 13

user connections via LAN, 50-52

user interface (UI) for server console, 53

UUIDs (universally unique identifiers), 53-55

V

vanilla servers

  advantages/disadvantages, 28-29

  agreeing to EULA, 34-35

  chat messages, console commands for, 55-58

  configuration files, 35-37

  console commands, 37-42

  finding online, 43-44

  giving items, console commands for, 59

  installing

   on Mac OS X, 31-33

   on Windows, 29-30

  Java environment preparation, 25

   JRE installation, 27-28

   verifying Java version, 26-27

  logfiles, 53-54

  managing with McMyAdmin, 65-68

  mapping IP address to hostname, 88-90

  meaning of term, 28, 34

  player connections, 86-87

  player discipline, console commands for, 59-64

  port forwarding configuration, 83-85

  running multiple instances, 42-43

  security, 90-91

  security issues, 76

  server console UI, 53

  server.properties file settings, 48-50

  teleportation, console commands for, 59

  test environment, 45-46

  testing port forwarding, 85-87

  user connections via LAN, 50-52

  UUIDs, 53-55

verifying Java version, 26-27

version numbers (SpigotMC)

  finding, 99-100

  changing, 104-105

view-distance property, 50

viewing

  file extensions, 31

  Minecraft Realms backups, 154

  player list, 56

  router configuration settings, 78-80

  TCP/IP configuration settings, 76-78

Village with Lots of Loot, 245

VIP plugin, 219-220

VIP server access/subscriptions, 219-220

virtual private servers (VPSs), 160

VoidLauncher, 135

Votifier, 240

voting, 232

VPSs (virtual private servers), 160

W

weather, starting/stopping rain, 40

WesterosCraft, 244

white-list property, 50

/whitelist console command, 63-64

whitelist servers, 15-16

Windows

finding IP addresses, 39

java - version command errors, 27

McMyAdmin installation, 66

startup scripts, 96

TCP/IP configuration settings, 76

vanilla server installation, 29-30

verifying Java version, 26

viewing file extensions, 31

WorldEdit, 102, 197-201, 240

WorldGuard, 101, 240

worlds

restoring in Minecraft Realms, 157

uploading to Minecraft Realms, 156-157

world spawn, 194

building spawn lobbies, 196-198

setting server spawn, 195

WorldEdit, 199-201

Wurst, 188

X-Y-Z

Xray Ultimate, 242

YAML file format, 98

YouTubers, top 10 Minecraft YouTubers, 243